LITERACY POWER

- WHAT A LAUGH!
- ON THE BRAIN
- VIEWING MEDIA
- NATURAL MYSTERIES
- TELLING THE STORY

Australia   Canada   Mexico   Singapore   Spain   United Kingdom   United States

Literacy Power C

Associate Vice President of Publishing
David Steele

Director of Publishing, Literacy and Reference
Joe Banel

Executive Managing Editor, Development
Darleen Rotozinski

Executive Managing Editor, Production
Nicola Balfour

Project Manager, Literacy
Diane Robitaille

Senior Project Editor
Patrice Peterkin

Proofreader
Sandy Manley

Editorial Assistants
Charlotte Martin
Lisa Peterson

Production Editor
Stacey Kauder

Production Coordinator
Franca Mandarino

Creative Director
Angela Cluer

Interior Modifications
Suzanne Peden

Cover Design
First Image

Cover Image
Kathy Ferguson-Johnson/
Photo Edit

Compositor
Pamela Clayton

Permissions/Photo Researcher
Lisa Brant

Printer
Transcontinental Printing Inc.

National Library of Canada Cataloguing in Publication Data
Literacy power C /
Patrice Peterkin,
Diane Robitaille, editors.

ISBN 0-7715-1085-3

1. English language—Textbooks. I. Peterkin, Patrice II. Robitaille, Diane

LB1576.L597 2005   428
C2005-900878-4

We wish to thank all those teachers, consultants, and students who contributed feedback during the developmental process of this series.

ISBN 0-7715-1085-3

Written, printed, and bound in Canada

Series Consultants E to H

Heather Birchall, Simcoe County DSB, ON
Breen Bernard, Durham DSB, ON
Susan Blocker, Thames Valley DSB, ON
Jo-Ann Carrothers, Hamilton-Wentworth, DSB, ON
Bill Chaisson, Corner Brook-Deer Lake-St. Barbe School Board District #3, NL
Robert Cutting, Durham, CDSB, ON
Owen Davis, London CDSB, ON
Becky Donaldson, Simcoe County DSB, ON
Tina Elliott, Hastings/Prince Edward DSB, ON
Lori Farren, School District 6, NB
Marg Frederickson, Burnaby School District 41, BC
Irene Heffel, Edmonton School District No. 7, AB
Jennifer Hunter, Thames Valley DSB, ON
Judith Hunter, Toronto DSB, ON
Maricel Ignacio, Independent Schools of Vancouver Archdiocese, BC
Ashley Kelly, York Region DSB, ON
Jinah Kim, York Region DSB, ON
Diana Knight, Halton DSB, ON
Eva Koskela, DSB One, Ontario Northeast, ON
Toni Kovach, Hamilton-Wentworth CDSB, ON
Tracy Kowalchuk, Hamilton-Wentworth DSB, ON
Linda Luedee, Corner Brook-Deer Lake-St. Barbe School Board District #3, NL

Stephanie Manderville, Hastings/Prince Edward DSB, ON
Gale May, York Region, DSB, ON
Ted McComb, Durham DSB, ON
Donna Nicholls, Parkland School Division No. 70, AB
Debra L. Northey, Trillium Lakelands DSB, ON
Sean O'Toole, Trillium Lakelands, DSB, ON
Mike Ouellette, Annapolis Valley Regional School Board, NS
Benjamin Paré, Burnaby School District 41, BC
Jennifer Perkin, CDSB of Eastern Ontario, ON
Robert Riel, Winnipeg School Division No.1, MB
Shirley Sewell, Lambton Kent DSB, ON
Tamar Stein, York Region DSB, ON
Christy Stewart, Avon-Maitland DSB, ON
Rosemary Stiglic, Peel District DSB, ON
James Stowe, Avalon East School District, NL
Michael Stubitsch, Toronto DSB, ON
Bill Talbot, Edmonton School District No. 7, AB
Mary Lynn Tolley, Waterloo CDSB, ON
Carolyn Van Alstyne, Trillium Lakelands DSB, ON
Ann Varty, Trillium Lakelands DSB, ON
Judy Wedeles, Halton DSB, ON
Peter Yan, Dufferin-Peel CDSB, ON
Catherine Zeisner, Thames Valley DSB, ON

Series Consultants A to D

Mary Adams, Thames Valley DSB, ON
Lori Austin, Dufferin Peel CDSB, ON
Lori Driussi, SD 41, BC
Denise Edwards, Toronto DSB, ON
Darlene Gordon, Sooke School District, BC
Charmaine Graves, Thames Valley DSB, ON
Phyllis Hildebrandt, Lakeshore DSB, ON
Luigi Iannacci, University of Western Ontario, ON

Sue Jackson, Thames Valley DSB, ON
Andrew Mildenberger, Toronto DSB, ON
Ken McDougall, Upper Grand DSB, ON
Janice Moore, St. Thomas University, NB
Darren Patterson, Calgary Board of Education, AB
Krista Pedersen, Upper Grand DSB, ON
Eric Wagner, Lakeview School Division, SK

✦ indicates Canadian content

UNIT 3: VIEWING MEDIA

UNIT 4: NATURAL MYSTERIES

For Genre/Format see Index on page 137

During Reading

A **sign** is a message that a company wants the whole community to read. Companies should make sure that their signs make sense or they'll end up in a book like *The Best of the World's Stupidest Signs*. Check out the following signs to find out how they ended up in that book.

Say What?

Signs from *The Best of the World's Stupidest Signs*
Collected by Michael O'Mara

1. a sign outside a store

2. no location given for sign, perhaps near a park

Goals at a Glance

clarifying meaning • small group discussion

HAVE YOUR EARS PIERCED

AND GET AN EXTRA PAIR TO TAKE HOME

3. a sign in a jewellery store

WE CAN REPAIR
ANYTHING

(Please knock hard on the door; the bell doesn't work.)

4. a sign on a repair-shop door

5. a sign in a safari park

6. a sign in a restaurant

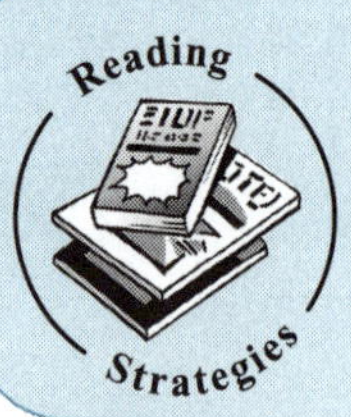

Reading for Information
- Read the text. Think about the information in it.
- Use a question mark (**?**) to mark any text that doesn't make sense.
- Use the information in the **captions** (the words beside or under an image that tell you about it) to help you understand the text.

Each question below matches a sign on page 2 or 3.
For example, question 1 is about sign 1. You can use <u>point form</u>
(a few words) to answer these questions.

1. How long does it really take to prepare photos: one hour or 20 minutes?

   ____

2. According to sign 2, who must drive slowly? _______________________

3. What do customers at the jewellery store get to take home?

   ____

4. What has the repair-shop owner **not** repaired?_____________________

5. a. What do you think a **safari park** is?_____________________________

   ____

   b. According to sign 5, who must stay in the car?__________________

6. How many days a week is the restaurant really open?________________

Extending: Ask your family and friends to share their favourite "stupid" signs with you. If they can't think of any, share the signs in this selection with them.

B Critical Thinking   *Clarifying Meaning*

1. Choose **one** sign on page 2 or 3.

2. Rewrite the sign so that it makes sense. The meaning should be clear,
   and the sign should not say the opposite of what it really means.

   ____

   ____

3. **a.** Ask a partner to read your new sign and check that it makes sense.

   b. Read your partner's sign and check that it makes sense.

C Oral Communication   *Small Group Discussion*

1. Get together with **three** classmates to discuss the signs from
   "Say What?" Try to answer the following questions:
   - Are the signs funny?
   - If so, what makes them funny?
   - Which sign is the funniest? Why?

2. Remember that some group members may have different opinions
   about whether the signs are funny or which sign is the funniest.
   Think about these opinions and how they affect your opinion
   about the signs.

Small Group Discussion
- Listen to what others are saying.
- Wait for your turn to speak.
- Stay on topic when you are speaking.

A comedian has to stand up in front of hundreds of people and **be funny**. With a partner, discuss whether this is a job you think you could do. Why or why not?

FOR THE BIRDS

Short Story by Robert Piotrowski

Some vacation this was turning out to be. Walter sat on the sand, stretched his legs out, and clicked together the toes of his flippered feet. A blister was already stinging his right heel. Just great. The boy let out a sigh. The sun beat on his back. Walter could feel it right through his T-shirt.

Goals at a Glance

reading for information • presenting a joke

"G'day."

The boy turned to face the voice. It belonged to a young girl about his age, tanned and golden-haired.

"Kids aren't allowed out here alone, you know," she said as she plopped down beside him.

"Yeah, I know. See that guy in the purple diving suit in the water?" He pointed to two people bobbing in the ocean a few hundred metres away. The girl nodded.

"That's my dad."

"Oh, I guess it's okay then. My name's Maria. You talk with an accent. Are you American?"

"Canadian. From Calgary," Walter said. "We're here on vacation."

"Are you staying at the resort?" Maria motioned to the tall buildings beyond the beach.

"Yes, until Saturday," the boy replied. "You know, the way you talk sounds funny to me too. You're Australian?"

The girl nodded again. "I've lived all my life in New South Wales. I know it like the inside of my diving mask. That woman teaching your dad to scuba is my mom. She's the diving instructor," Maria said proudly. "So, how do you like your holiday here so far?"

"It's okay I guess. Not great," Walter admitted.

"You don't like diving?" Maria asked with surprise.

"Not so much." The boy shrugged. "I'm not into outdoor stuff."

"What do you like to do?" Maria asked.

"I don't know. Stuff," he answered with a shrug.

"Like what?" Maria persisted.

Walter wondered if he should tell Maria. Would she take him seriously? Most people didn't. Finally, he admitted, "Jokes."

"Jokes?" Maria asked, puzzled.

"Yeah. You know, like riddles and stuff. I even make them up myself," Walter confided.

"Are they funny?" she asked.

"Sure they're funny. Like, what comes from outer space, is silver and round, and smells awful?" Walter used his "telling-a-joke" voice.

"I don't know," Maria finally gave up.

"An unidentified flying armpit!" Walter shouted.

Maria burst into giggles. Walter smiled.

"I like that one," Maria told him.

"Thanks. I'm going to be a comedian when I grow up," Walter admitted.

"I'm going to be a diving instructor like Mom" Maria said. "I helped her lead a dive last week. Right now I'm saving up for a new set of flippers."

"I'm saving up too," Walter said. "I'm saving up all my jokes for when I get older. That's when I can really be a comedian."

"Why wait until then?" Maria asked, thinking she would hate to wait until she was an adult before she could dive again.

"I don't know," the boy admitted. "To be a comedian you need an audience that's ready to laugh at your jokes."

"So find an audience."

Walter smiled at the notion of just finding an audience, like you might find a loonie on the sidewalk. "Where?"

"Right here," the girl announced.

"Yeah, sure," Walter said doubtfully.

"Seriously." Maria stood up and brushed the sand off her shorts. "Come on."

"Where to?" Walter looked up at Maria. He had to squint to keep the sun out of his eyes.

"To an audience. A special one. Australian style," Maria said over her shoulder, already heading down the beach.

"An audience?" Walter scrambled to keep up.

"Yeah. Come on! You're just sitting here doing nothing anyway," she called. "What have you got to lose?"

The boy followed his new friend across the hot sand. A few minutes later they reached a patch of palm trees and bushes.

Maria stopped. She appeared to be looking around for something specific. When she didn't find it, she led Walter to another clump of bushes. After two more tries, she was finally satisfied and told him to go ahead.

For the Birds   **9**

"Go ahead with what?" Walter asked, looking around, puzzled.

"Your jokes. Tell some jokes to your audience," Maria explained.

"What audience?" he asked. "There's nobody else here. This is strictly for the birds."

"Right. Just do it," Maria insisted.

"All right." Walter took a deep breath, and began, "What do you get when you cross Australia's most famous animal with a glass of milk? Give up? A kanga-mooo!"

Maria chuckled. Her laughter was echoed by a cackling in the bushes. It sounded like "Ooh-ooh-ooh-ooh-ooh-ooh-ooh-ooh-ooh-ooh-ooh-ooh!"

The mysterious laughter grew louder before disappearing.

"They liked it!" Maria yelled, breaking the sudden silence.

Walter was stunned. "They sure did. B-But who are they?"

"Kookaburras," Maria explained.

Walter shook his head. "Who?"

"What, not who. Kookaburras. They're birds that sound like they're laughing when they sing. They're your audience, and they think you're funny." Maria pointed. Walter spotted a bird in a patch of grassy leaves. It was brownish and about the size of a bike seat.

"That's my audience? Cool!" Walter exclaimed.

"They can't really understand what you're saying. But it's good practice. Tell another joke," Maria encouraged her new friend.

"Why did the car think its driver was a bully?" the boy asked. "Because he was always hitting the brakes!"

Again the kookaburras cackled, louder than before.

"See," Maria teased, "Australia is pretty good for just about everything."

"Pretty good? What are you talking about? I love this place!" Walter declared.

And with that, the boy began telling more jokes and riddles. He went through all the jokes he had. When he reached the end and could not remember any more, he started over from the very beginning.

Maria's giggles eventually turned into great big belly laughs, with the kookaburras joining in. They laughed and giggled together as the sun set on the yellow Australian beach.

1. a. Circle the words that **best** describe Walter.

Words to Describe Walter				
funny	shy	serious	creative	bold
smart	worried	happy	ambitious	unimaginative

b. Explain why you chose these words. Use evidence from the selection to support your answers.

____

____

____

c. Cross out the words you think **don't** describe Walter.

2. a. Circle the words that **best** describe Maria.

Words to Describe Maria				
friendly	shy	practical	sensible	bold
smart	worried	happy	ambitious	unimaginative

b. Explain why you chose these words. Use evidence from the selection to support your answers.

____

____

____

c. Cross out the words you think **don't** describe Maria.

3. Would you rather have Walter or Maria for a best friend? Explain why.

____

____

____

B Oral Communication *Presenting a Joke*

Follow these steps to present a joke to a small group.

1. Choose a joke from the selection or from another source.
   In your notebook, write down the joke. Leave lots of space
   around the joke to make notes.

2. Practise reading the joke aloud several times.
   Experiment with **volume**, **tone**, and **pace**. In your notebook,
   make notes to help you remember what worked best.

3. Tell the joke to a small group of people (classmates, friends, or family).

4. In your notebook, record who your audience was and how your
   audience responded to the joke.

Presenting a Joke

- Change the **volume** of your voice to suit the joke. You might whisper
  some parts of the joke and shout other parts.
- Experiment with the **tone** of your voice: high, low, angry, or sad.
- Check that the **pace** (how quickly you speak and when you pause)
  suits the joke.

For the Birds **13**

- A **sentence** is a group of words that tells or asks something.
  A sentence expresses a complete thought.
    EXAMPLES: The boy let out a sigh. We're here on vacation.

- A sentence begins with a capital letter. A sentence can end in a period,
  question mark, or exclamation mark.
    EXAMPLES: That's my dad. Are you American? That's so cool!

---

1. Read the following groups of words. Put a check mark (✓) beside every
   sentence. Put an **X** beside any group of words that is **not** a sentence.

   a. Long, long ago. _____

   b. My name is Maria. _____

   c. Walter sat on the sand. _____

   d. Just great. _____

   e. Are you staying at the hotel? _____

2. For each group of words above that you put an **X** beside, add details
   to make it a complete sentence. Write the sentences below.

   ____

   ____

   ____

TIPS

Sentences

- Sometimes an author creates a sentence using a group of words
  that does not express a complete thought.
    EXAMPLE: From Calgary, Alberta.

Sentences that are not complete sound like how people really speak.

- Don't use sentences that are not complete in formal writing, such as
  reports or speeches.

- A **synonym** is a word that has the same or almost the same meaning as another word.

    EXAMPLE: **Useful** and **helpful** are synonyms.

- Writers use synonyms so that all their sentences don't sound the same.

1. Reread page 10 of the story. Circle two words that the author used instead of the word **said**.

2. Reread the last page of the story. Underline **two** words that the author used instead of the word **laughed**.

3. Choose **two** of the following words. Look the words up in a thesaurus (or use the thesaurus function on a computer). For each word you chose, list at least **three** synonyms to replace that word.

   a. say ______________ ______________ ______________

   b. laugh ______________ ______________ ______________

   c. walk ______________ ______________ ______________

   d. stunned ______________ ______________ ______________

   e. alone ______________ ______________ ______________

   f. special ______________ ______________ ______________

Extending: Get together with **two** classmates who chose different words. Together, write another story about Maria or Walter. Use the original words above and the synonyms you found.

TIPS

Synonyms

- Use synonyms to replace overused words (like **said** or **nice**).
- Make sure that you understand the meaning of the synonym.
- Check that the new word works in the sentence.

Before Reading
"Palindromania!"

Have you ever met someone whose name reads the same way forward and backward, like BOB or ANNA? Write BOB or ANNA forward and backward and check it out.

Words that read the same both ways are called **palindromes**. Sometimes an entire sentence looks the same when spelled in different directions, like "PUT IT UP." Try writing all the words in that sentence both forward and backward.

Jon Agee is a famous artist and writer. In this selection, he's used his interest in palindromes to create some funny comic strips. Look at the title of the selection, "Palindromania!" What do you think **palindromania** means?

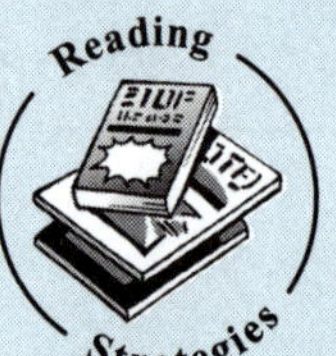

Comic Strips

- For each comic strip, look at the **pictures** and read the **text**.
- Think about the story the comic strip tells.
- In most comic strips, you'll also want to think about what you know about the characters. For example, what you know about Calvin from the *Calvin and Hobbes* comic strip can help you understand a new comic strip.

Fast Fact

The word **aibohphobia** describes a fear of palindromes!

PALINDROMANIA!

Comic Strips from *Palindromania!* by Jon Agee

FURTHER READING

If you liked this selection, look for more books by **Jon Agee**
at your local library. Here are just a few titles:
* *Go Hang a Salami! I'm a Lasagna Hog! and Other Palindromes*
* *So Many Dynamos! and Other Palindromes*
* *Sit on a Potato Pan, Otis! MORE Palindromes*
* *Who Ordered the Jumbo Shrimp? and Other Oxymorons*
* *Elvis Lives! and Other Anagrams*

1. Check off the words or phrases below that are palindromes.
If you need to, use the space provided to write the words backward.

❏ PAY DAY ____

❏ RADAR ____

❏ WAS IT A CAT I SAW? ____________________________________

❏ WAS IT A DOG I SAW? ____________________________________

❏ KAYAK ____

❏ STOP POTS ____

❏ NEIL, AN ALIEN ____

❏ GOOD DOG ____

❏ STAR SEES RATS ____

❏ TEN ANIMALS I SLAM IN A NET ____________________________

2. Choose **one palindrome** from above. Create a drawing for that
palindrome. Use Jon Agee's work as a model.

1. **a.** Which comic strip from "Palindromania!" do you like best?
Put a check mark (✓) beside that comic strip.

   b. Explain why you like that comic strip.

   ____

   ____

   ____

   c. If you think the comic strip is funny, explain what makes it funny.

   ____

   ____

   ____

Reflecting

2. **a.** Put a question mark (?) beside any comic strip that you don't
understand.

   b. With a partner, discuss that comic strip.

   c. Did talking about the comic strip help you understand it? Explain.

   ____

   ____

   ____

- Words in a sentence are in an order that makes the meaning clear.
    EXAMPLE: I saw a cat.

- In a question, the order is slightly different.
    EXAMPLE: Was it a cat I saw?
            OR
            Did I see a cat?

- To make a palindrome, sometimes the writer has to reverse the natural order of a sentence.
    EXAMPLE: Ten animals I slam in a net. (Natural order: I slam ten animals in a net.)

Arrange these words in an order that makes the meaning clear. Remember to add a capital letter to the beginning and a period or question mark to the end of the sentence.

1. cat have I a ______________________________________

2. drank we juice ______________________________________

3. listen music let's to ______________________________________

4. to going the zoo we are ______________________________________

5. book that is reading she ______________________________________

6. yesterday a movie watched we ______________________________________

7. at the library when meeting we are ______________________________________

8. my report book due today is ______________________________________

9. book great a reading I'm ______________________________________

10. for dinner tomorrow over come ______________________________________

During Reading
"Three Funny Poems"

There are **three** poems on the next three pages.
For each poem, use the reading strategy below.

1. For the poem "The Hardest Thing," read the poem
   silently to yourself once. Next, **read** the poem **aloud**
   with feeling.

2. For the poem "Advice," read the poem silently to
   yourself. As you read, **visualize** what the poem is
   describing. When you **visualize**, you are picturing
   something in your mind.

3. For the poem "NO," **listen** as your teacher reads you
   the poem. **Think** about the rhythm and rhyme in
   the poem.

Vocabulary

loitering: standing around doing nothing

skinny-dipping: swimming without clothes on

fly rod casters: people who fish with a long fishing
pole that throws out a long length of fishing line

heavers: throwers

Three Funny Poems

Poems by various poets

The Hardest Thing

Poem by Judith Viorst

If you think that the hardest thing is saying you're wrong
    when you've been wrong,
I think you should know
That the really hardest thing is, when you've been absolutely
    right,
Not saying nyah nyah nyah, I told you so.

Advice

Poem by James Stevenson

IF YOU ALWAYS WALK
→ STRAIGHT AHEAD
YOU'LL PROBABLY MISS
WHAT'S JUST
AROUND THE
CORNER

NO

Poem by Shel Silverstein

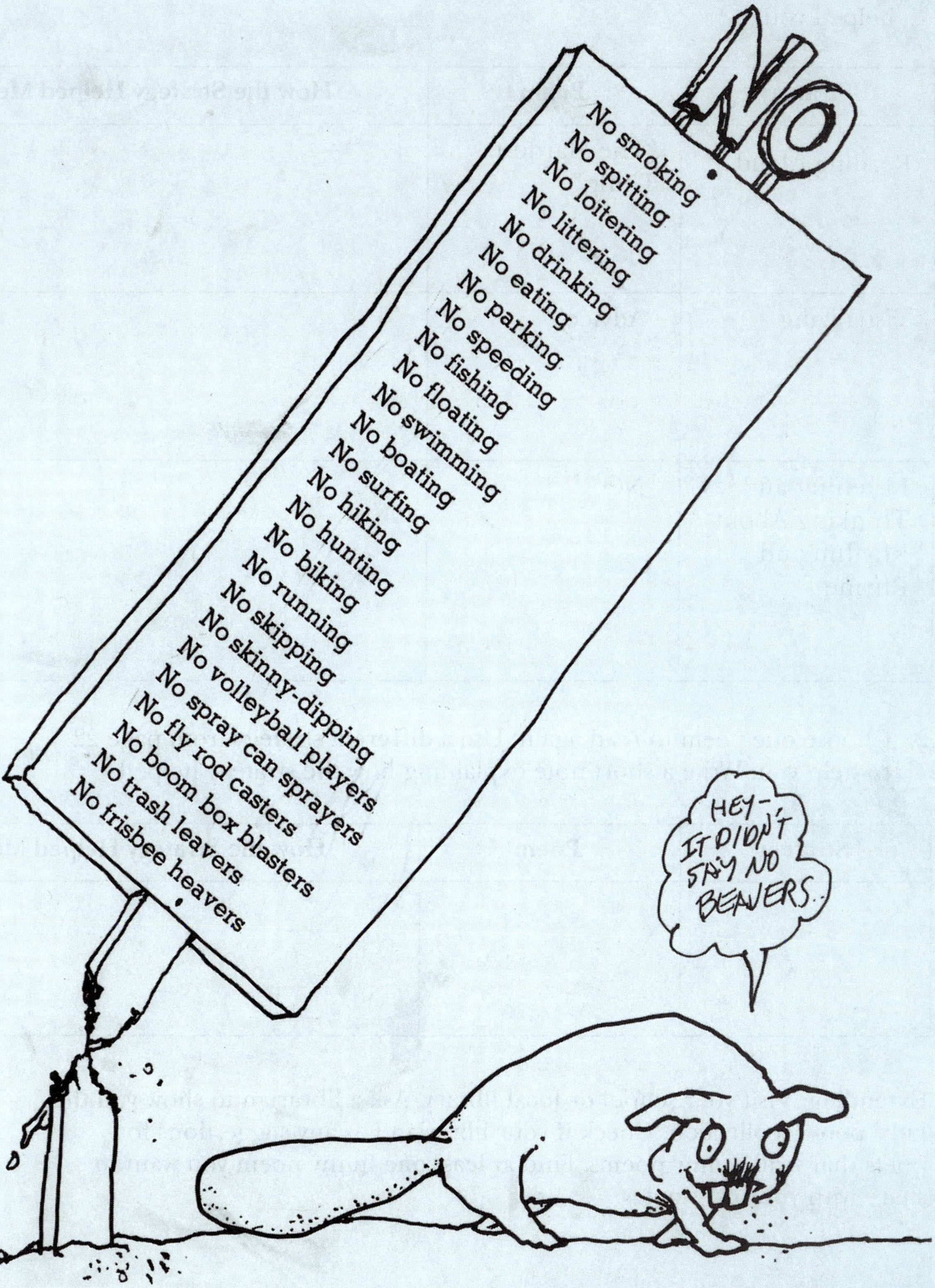

Three Funny Poems **25**

1. The During Reading activity on page 22 asked you to use **three** different strategies to read the poems. Think about how each strategy helped you understand the poem. Write a short note explaining how the strategy helped you.

Strategy	Poem	How the Strategy Helped Me
Reading Aloud	"The Hardest Thing"	
Visualizing	"Advice"	
Listening and Thinking About Rhythm and Rhyme	"NO"	

2. Choose **one** poem to read again. Use a **different** strategy from page 22 to help you. Write a short note explaining how the strategy helped.

Strategy	Poem	How the Strategy Helped Me

Extending: Visit your school or local library. Ask a librarian to show you the kids' poetry collection. Check if your librarian has any suggestions for poets that write funny poems. Find at least **one** funny poem you want to share with your classmates.

B Critical Thinking *Making Judgments*

1. Which of the **three** poems do you think is the funniest?
   Rank the poems from funny to funniest.

   Funny Poem ____

   Funnier Poem ____

   Funniest Poem ____

2. Get together with a small group and discuss how you all ranked
   the poems. Did everyone in the group rank the poems the same way?
   Explain to your group why you ranked the poems the way you did.

3. With your group, discuss what makes a poem funny.
   Take notes during the discussion.

C Oral Communication *Presenting a Poem*

Follow these steps to present <u>one</u> poem to a small group.

1. Choose **one** poem to read aloud to a small group.

2. Read the poem silently several times until you understand
   what the poet is trying to say.

3. Practise reading the poem aloud. Experiment with your volume, tone,
   and pace. Make notes in the margin beside the poem to show how you
   will read it.

4. Present your poem to a small group.

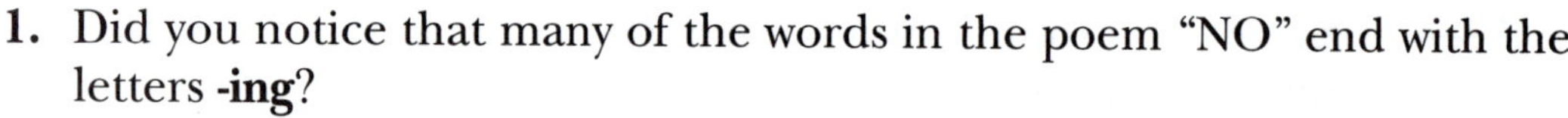

Vocabulary *Word Endings*

1. Did you notice that many of the words in the poem "NO" end with the letters **-ing**?

smoking	spitting	loitering	littering	drinking	eating	parking
speeding	fishing	floating	swimming	boating	surfing	hiking
hunting	biking	running	skipping	skinny-dipping		

2. Sort the words in the box into the following **three** categories. (Hint: Circle the original part of the word, for example, smok(ing.)

Words Ending in -ing Where the Spelling Doesn't Change	Words Ending in -ing Where the -e Is Dropped	Words Ending in -ing Where the Final Consonant Is Doubled

3. Suggest at least **three** new **-ing** words you would add to this poem.

_______________ _______________ _______________

4. What else did you notice about the words in this poem?

____

____

Self-Assessment *Oral Communication*

1. Check off the oral communication activities you completed during this unit:

   ❑ Small Group Discussion (page 5)
   ❑ Presenting a Joke (page 13)
   ❑ Presenting a Poem (page 27)

2. Describe **one** thing that worked really well when you completed **one** of these activities.

   ____

   ____

3. Set a goal for the next time you complete a similar activity. How will you improve your work?

   ____

   ____

Project Idea *Preparing a Comedy Show*

Follow these steps to prepare a comedy show.

Step 1. Work with a small group to collect material for the comedy show. You'll need jokes, riddles, and funny poems. Think about how you might present comic strips or signs in your show.

Step 2. With your group, sort through the material you've collected. As a group, make some decisions.
- What material will you want to use?
- How will you present each item? (Return to pages 13 and 27 for some tips.)
- Who will present it? (Each group member should present **one** item.)

Step 3. With the whole class, plan the comedy show. Make sure each group is doing different material. Decide in what order the groups will present.

Step 4. Perform your comedy show for another class or family members.

These are the <u>three</u> most important points to remember during a small group discussion.

- <u>Listen</u> to what others are saying.

- <u>Wait</u> for your turn to speak.

- <u>Stay on topic</u> when you are speaking.

To see these points in action, read this discussion about planning a comedy show.

Listen to Others

Wait for Your Turn

Stay on Topic

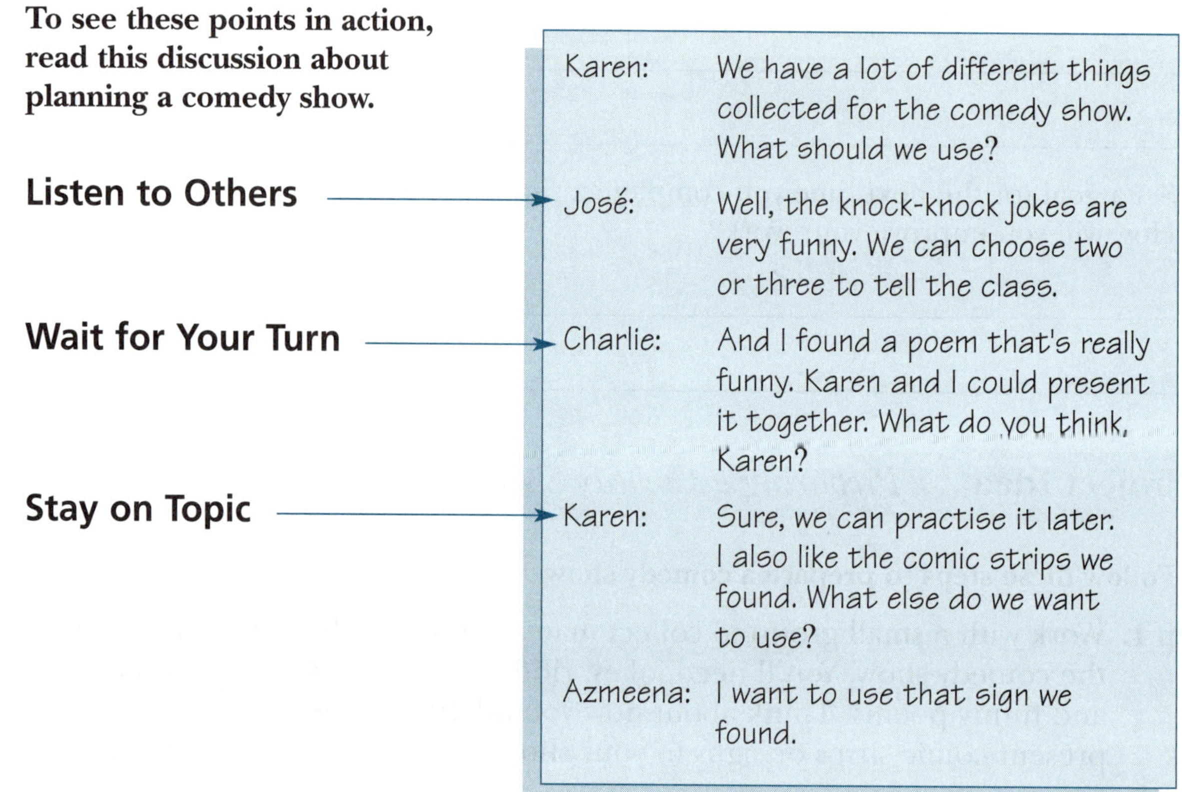

Before Reading
"Feed Your Brain!"

Write down **four** foods that are good for you. Think about why these foods are healthy.

Food	Why This Food Is Healthy

Reading With a Purpose

Think about your **purpose** when you read. Sometimes, you may read just for pleasure. At other times, you will read a text to get information (like this selection).

- Read each paragraph. Then stop to think about the information in it.
- Use the information in the title, by-line, images, and captions to help you read the text.

Vocabulary

iodine: a chemical used in medicine and photography

flaxseeds: seeds from a herb plant

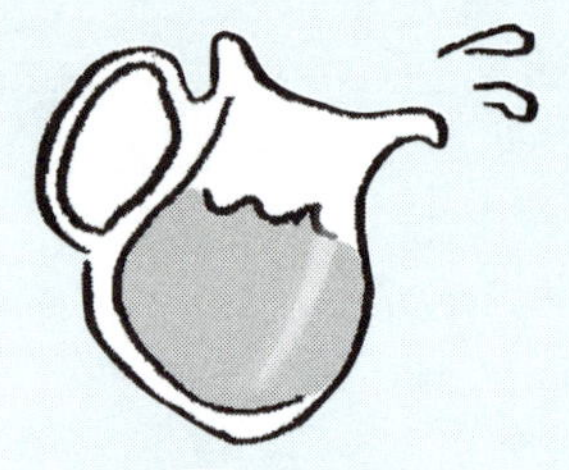    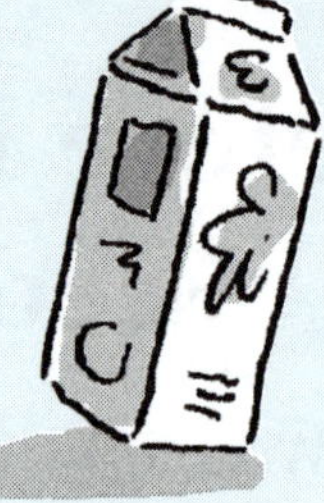

Feed Your Brain!

Facts by Dr. Jorge Diez

- Almonds, spinach, chicken, and milk are all foods that are good for the brain.

- Remember to drink lots of water or juice the day of a test. Your memory needs water or juice to work best.

- Eat lots of vegetables to improve your memory and brain power. Raw or lightly cooked vegetables are better for your brain than overcooked vegetables.

- Are you having trouble concentrating? Are you stressed about a test? Eat some Brazil nuts or sunflower seeds to help you concentrate!

- Are you feeling sad or tired? You might not have enough <u>iodine</u> in your diet, or your brain may not be getting enough blood. Twice a week, eat some ocean fish, like tuna, sardines, or mackerel, to keep your brain working at full speed. If you don't like fish or can't eat it, try <u>flaxseeds</u>, dark green, leafy vegetables, or seaweed.

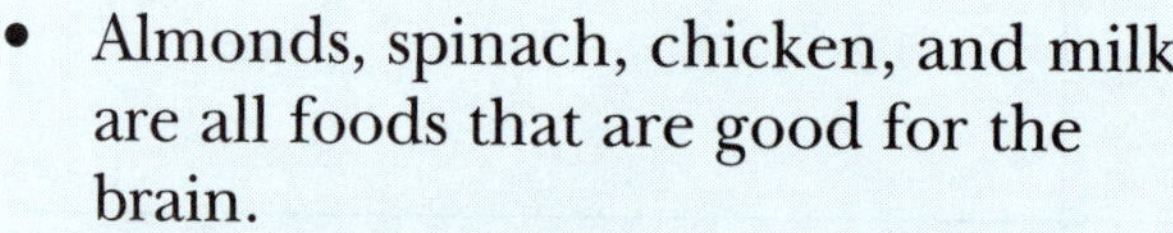

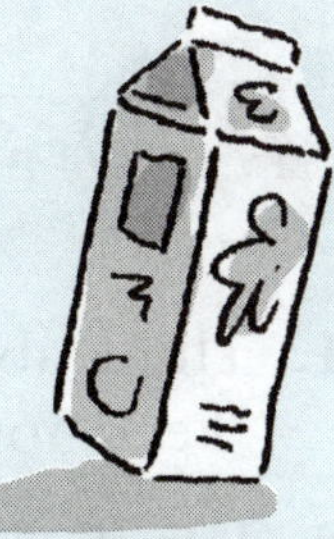

The Amazing Brain: More Facts

- Your brain is like a huge phone system, sending messages between billions of cell phones, er, cells. Imagine everyone in the world talking on the phone at the same time and that each person is talking to 10 000 other people. That's how much activity is going on in your brain right now!

- Lots of people can't remember information they've just read. Some brain experts believe that's because too often the information is presented with black type on a white background. Most brains work better when information can be connected with lots of colours and images. For example, if you are trying to remember the French word for **pig** (*cochon*), you might think of a large pink couch with a pink pig lying on it. (*Cochon* even sounds a bit like **couch**, so that also helps you remember it.)

> "Minds are like parachutes;
> they work better when open."
> —**Thomas Dewar**

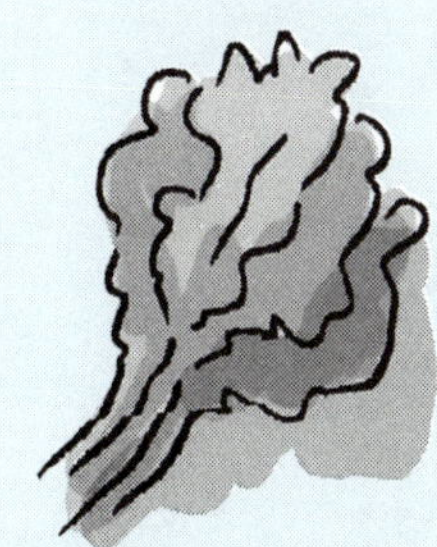

Feed Your Brain!

1. Think about what you learned by reading the selection "Feed Your Brain!"

2. Use the chart below to organize the information from page 32.

Categories	Food or Drink
Good for the Brain	
Good for the Memory	
Good for Concentration	
Good for an Energy Boost or To Make You Feel Happy	

3. **a.** There are **three** items on page 33 (two brain facts and one quotation). Suggest how **one** of these items could be shown in a visual way (with a chart, diagram, or picture).

   ____

   b. Discuss your idea with a partner or small group.

   c. Together, choose **one** way to show **one** of these items. Put that idea into action in the box below. If you need more space, use another piece of paper.

Work with a partner to complete these activities. Take turns putting your memory to the test and checking each other's answers.

1. Read the following lists of words. Cover the **last two** words in each list and try to complete the list from memory.

   a. girl   chocolate   phone

   b. pants   house   computer

   c. pizza   basement   basketball

   d. book   lamp   couch

> **Tip:** Use the words to make up an interesting sentence and repeat it in your head.
>
> EXAMPLE: The girl sold chocolate cookies over the phone.

2. **a.** Now imagine you are going shopping. Memorize the following list of foods that you need to buy. You have **two** minutes.

   spaghetti sauce

   spaghetti

   bread

   cereal

   milk

   b. After **two** minutes, cover the list. Try to repeat all **five** items to yourself.

   c. Now try again, but this time make up a funny story to help you remember all of the items.

   EXAMPLE: The spaghetti sauce came out of the spaghetti volcano and covered the town of Bread and Cereal with hot milk.

> **Tip:** One way to remember the list is to imagine a grocery store. Imagine yourself walking along the aisles and picture the items on the shelves.

3. Review the strategies that you used to remember the lists. How do you think these strategies will be helpful in your life?

____

____

Another way to increase your brain power is to complete activities like the following.

1. Cross out the word that does not belong in each group.
   Give yourself **30 seconds**.

a. green	yellow	small
b. weak	strong	muscle
c. dentist	teach	doctor
d. above	over	umbrella
e. leg	nose	arm

   Answers
   a. small b. muscle c. teach
   d. umbrella e. nose

2. A **synonym** is a word that means the same as another word.
   Circle the synonym of the **bold** word in each list.
   Give yourself **30 seconds**.

a. stop	start	halt	break
b. large	big	small	average
c. help	hurt	aid	send
d. stay	come	remain	leave
e. scary	funny	chilly	frightening

   Answers
   a. halt b. big c. aid
   d. remain e. frightening

3. An **antonym** is a word that means the opposite of another word.
   Circle the antonym of the **bold** word in each list.
   Give yourself **30 seconds**.

a. short	long	tiny	small
b. open	unlock	close	unwrap
c. happy	glad	sad	joyful
d. come	go	send	arrive
e. truth	secret	fact	lie

   Answers
   a. long b. close c. sad
   d. go e. lie

D Researching *Locating Resources*

Follow these steps to find out the health benefits of <u>one</u> of the foods below.

1. Choose **one** food to research:

   ❑ almonds   ❑ spinach

   ❑ chicken   ❑ milk

   ❑ fruit juice   ❑ Brazil nuts

   ❑ sunflower seeds   ❑ tuna (or other fish)

   ❑ flaxseed   ❑ seaweed

2. Look for information about the health benefits of the food you chose. Find at least **two** different sources of information (a book and a magazine, for example). See the strategies below for suggestions about the types of resources you might use.

3. Record at least **three** facts you learn from your research.

   ____

   ____

   ____

   ____

   ____

4. Share your facts with students who have researched other foods.

Extending: With the class, develop a list of the top **five** healthiest foods. Decide which foods on the list are the healthiest. Make sure you all agree on the foods you choose.

Or, you could develop a poster or commercial to advertise the health benefits of the food you researched.

Locating Resources

- Visit the school or public library. Use the library's computer or card catalogue to look for nonfiction books on your topic.
- Check health-food magazines, brochures, or pamphlets at a health food, drug, or grocery store.

Feed Your Brain! **37**

Before Reading
"Vision Quest"

Step 1. The words in this chart come from the selection "Vision Quest." Read these words. Think about what each word means. Think about how all the words are connected.

Words From the Selection	What All of These Words Make Me Think of
vision quest	
fasting	
spirits	
Aboriginal	
elders	

Step 2. What do **all** of these words make you think of? Record your ideas in the second column of the chart.

During Reading

As you read, put a check mark (✓) beside the paragraph that tells you what a **vision quest** is.

Vision Quest

Personal Account by Ron Geyshick

Every spring, my family would head out onto the ice around the middle of April and stay for a month, <u>trapping</u>. We'd be back by the first week of May.

I was nine years old when I started my fasting. My dad told me a story about what to do on a vision quest and how he'd done it. It was exciting to hear, and I was really interested. I wondered if I could do that myself. For at least a couple of days before I started, he gave me medicine, something to drink. Then he took me to an island. The ice had just gone out of Jean Lake a couple of days before, and the weather was nice.

My dad told me, "Pick up your rabbit-fur blanket and your deerskin mattress, that's all. Nothing else. I'm going to leave you alone on this island for four days and four nights. While I'm gone, don't drink any water or chew twigs. At nighttime, if you get cold, pick up a flat rock and put it on your chest. Keep it there until you get warm. If you get cold during the day, run around the island a few times until you warm up."

Goals at a Glance

asking questions • writing a personal account

I did exactly what he told me. It was cold in the mornings just before the sun came up. That's when I ran and lifted rocks. The first year, I didn't hear any spirits at all. For four days and four nights, the only sound I heard was from my grumbling stomach.

Ask Yourself

Do you think you could do what Ron did? Why or why not?

The next year, I fasted again. This second year, it wasn't too hard for me. I wasn't so hungry. I was full of excitement. On the second night I stayed on the island, I heard strange voices. I almost felt like I was crazy. The trees began to talk, telling stories to each other, about places that they'd been today and other places they'd go to tomorrow. They named a few places I know, so I believed them.

When the third year came, I was looking forward to it. My fasting was full of dreams and visions. I don't want to go into every detail of my vision quest. I'll try to keep the story short and simple, and skip a lot of things.

Ask Yourself

What personal qualities do you think Ron must have had to complete a vision quest?

Finally my fourth year came. I began to travel with the spirits, around the world in four directions, to see places. Last year, when Brian and I drove to Saskatoon, I recognized a few places I'd seen long before on my vision quest.

So this is the way I learned how to be an Aboriginal; how I learned medicines, which is what I wanted most. I learned to know different animals and spirits, and I enjoyed them very much. I was more afraid of my own people than I felt about spirits. I don't like to go into crowds, and I also don't like to walk on people's trails. I learned to obey my parents' orders, and respect my elders' stories, for the understanding I received.

Ask Yourself
Do you think the vision quests have been positive events in Ron's life? Support your answer with evidence from the selection.

A **Understanding the Selection** *Demonstrating Understanding*

1. What is a vision quest?______________________________

____

____

2. In your opinion, why would someone go on a vision quest?

____

____

B **Critical Thinking** *Asking Questions*

1. Think of **two** questions Ron might want to ask his father before starting his first vision quest.

____

____

2. Think of **two** questions the father might want to ask Ron after Ron's first vision quest.

____

____

3. Think of **two** questions you would like to ask Ron about vision quests.

____

____

4. Exchange your questions with a partner's questions. Don't try to answer these questions. Just think about how the questions give you a deeper insight or offer a new perspective into the selection.

Writing *A Personal Account*

- A personal account may be written to explain how certain events affected the writer. The audience may or may not be people the writer knows.

Follow these steps to write a personal account about an event in your life.

1. Think about an important event in your life. In your notebook, briefly note the details of that event. Include a sentence about how this event affected you.

2. Make a decision about who you want your audience to be: classmates, friends, family members, or your teacher.

3. Write a personal account that is at least **five** paragraphs long. The planner below will help you.

Personal Account Planner

Introduction (one paragraph)
Briefly introduce
the important event.

Body (three paragraphs)
Provide details about
- what happened
- who was involved
- where and when the
  event occurred
- why it happened
- how it made you feel

Conclusion (one paragraph)
Explain why the
event is important.

4. Give your personal account a title. Add an illustration.

- A **verb** is a word that shows action or a state of being.
  EXAMPLES: I <u>started</u> fasting. He <u>feels</u> fine.

- Verbs have different **tenses** that tell **when** an action takes place.

- The **past tense** tells you that something happened in the past.
  EXAMPLES: My dad <u>told</u> me a story. It <u>was</u> exciting to hear.

- The **present tense** tells you what is happening now.
  EXAMPLE: I <u>start</u> my vision quest today.

- The **future tense** tells you about something that will happen.
  EXAMPLE: I <u>will tell</u> you the story tonight.

1. Write **present**, **past**, or **future** to tell the tense of each <u>underlined</u> verb.

   a. Ron <u>went</u> on a vision quest. _______________________

   b. Ron <u>thinks</u> the rules are easy. ____________ _______

   c. He <u>will go</u> on another vision quest next year. _______________________

2. **a.** In your notebook, write **one** sentence about yourself
   in the past tense.

   b. Write **one** sentence about yourself in the present tense.

   c. Write **one** sentence about yourself in the future tense.

TIPS

Verbs and Verb Tenses

- When you're writing, try to choose as specific a verb as possible to describe the action. "**Walking** around the block" is not the same as "**strolling** around the block."

- Try to use the same tense within one piece of writing. If you've started a story in the past tense, it should end in the past tense.

Before Reading

When you're a kid, you're afraid of the dark or a monster under the bed. What happens when you get a bit older? What's the most terrifying thing to you?

In this speech, high school student Katia Hildebrandt talks about her worst fear.

Fear

Speech by Katia Hildebrandt

If you haven't experienced it, you don't know what it's like. Let me explain.

It's like jumping off a 500-m cliff. Or possibly more like discovering you have a horrible, skin-eating disease. Not getting it yet? Imagine being strapped to a bed while rats run across your body. Or standing naked in a room full of clothed people.

Ask Yourself
Reread the first **two** paragraphs. What do you think the word **it** refers to in the first two paragraphs?

It's definitely a full-body experience. Your stomach feels like you've just swallowed a litre of acid. Your legs shake. Your head pounds with the millions of thoughts rushing through it. Your voice box has been ripped out, played with, and then stepped on by a herd of wild beasts. The same goes for your heart after it bursts from your chest because it's beating so hard. And on top of it all, you're probably starting to cry.

Goals at a Glance

responding personally • thinking about speeches

I'm not saying that it's the worst feeling in the world. But while you're experiencing it, you usually think so. When all those eyes are staring at you, boring holes through your skin, you can't help but feel that way, unless, of course, you're not cursed with this unfortunate phobia.

I'm not talking about a fear of snakes or high places. I'm not even talking about a fear of exams. Ladies and gentlemen, excuse me while I pass out. I have stage fright.

A Critical Thinking   *Responding Personally*

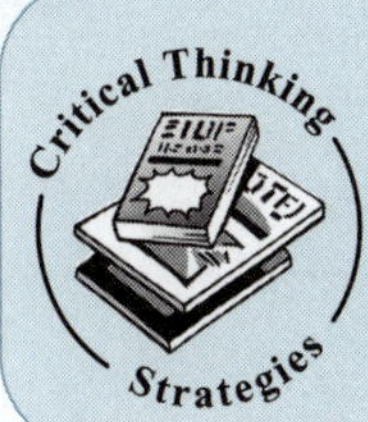

Responding Personally

When you **respond personally** to a text, you explore your thoughts and feelings about it.

- Question the writer's ideas. Think about your own opinions or ideas.
- Think about your response to the text and why you responded that way.

1. Reread the selection.

2. Beside each paragraph, record your response to it.
   Use the points in the strategy box to help you.

3. With a partner, compare your responses to the text.

B Writer's Craft   *Thinking About Speeches*

1. Read the following list of criteria for a good speech:

   ❑ A good speech is short and to the point.
   ❑ A good speech is clear and does **not** confuse the listener.
   ❑ A good speech makes connections between the listener and the speaker.
   ❑ A good speech uses writing techniques such as repetition, humour,
      or emotional language.

2. Reread "Fear." Check off the criteria that you believe this speech meets.

3. In your notebook, write a short paragraph assessing "Fear."
   Refer to each of the criteria above and give reasons for
   your assessment. End your paragraph by explaining whether
   or not you feel that "Fear" is a good speech.

 **Writing**   *A Speech*

1. Write **three** paragraphs describing what you are afraid of. If you aren't afraid of anything, write **five** paragraphs describing how great it is to be fearless!

First Paragraph

Describe what you are afraid of.

Second Paragraph

Explain how you feel when you encounter what you fear.

Third Paragraph

Describe how you try to avoid what you fear.

2. Think about how you can turn your paragraphs into a speech. You may need to add an introductory or concluding paragraph.

3. Use the criteria of a good speech (see activity B) to help you write your speech.

4. When you've written your speech, read it aloud to hear how it sounds. Use the following checklist to assess your speech. My speech:

   ❑ is short and to the point
   ❑ is clear and does **not** confuse the listener
   ❑ makes connections between the listener and the speaker
   ❑ uses techniques such as repetition, humour, or emotional language

Extending: Decide whether you will present your speech to the whole class, to a small group, or just your teacher. Ask your audience to assess your speech using the criteria in activity B. Make changes to your speech based on your audience's feedback.

Language Conventions   *Nouns*

> - **Nouns** are naming words. A noun names a person, place, thing, or idea.
>   EXAMPLES: ladies, cliff, stomach, fear

1. **Fear** is a noun that names an idea. List **three** other nouns that
name ideas.

__________________ __________________ __________________

2. Use the nouns you listed in question 1 to write **three** sentences.

____

____

____

3. In the chart below, write **three** sentences about a time you spoke in
front of a large group.

4. Sort the nouns you've used into **four** categories: **person**, **place**,
thing, or **idea**.

Sentence	Person	Place	Thing	Idea

During Reading

As you read this solve-it-yourself mystery, highlight the clues
the author gives. Make notes in the margin to help you solve the mystery.

Pizza Puzzle

Solve-It-Yourself Mystery from *Super Sleuth* by Jackie Vivelo

I had reached the corner of the street where I live
when I saw Danny Dinello. He delivers pizza for his
dad. His little blue car with the picture of the pizza
on the door was pulled onto the grass. The door was
open on the driver's side, and Danny was sitting
there looking confused.

"Hi, Danny," I called. "Is something wrong?"

"Yeah, there is," Danny answered. "Hey, aren't you
Ellen Sloan?"

Goals at a Glance

drawing conclusions • making connections

"Yes, I am. Can I help you?"

"Maybe you could at that. I have three pizzas to deliver, and I have three names and addresses. But the delivery slips got shuffled. I don't know which order goes where."

"Maybe I can help," I offered.

I asked Danny for the names of the people he was supposed to deliver to. He read them to me, and I copied them down in my notebook: Mr. Burks, Mrs. Adler, and Mr. Harris.

"Tell me everything you remember about the orders," I suggested.

"I took two of the orders myself, and Dad took the other call. If I could just remember the orders I took, it would help. But it's no use. I've thought about it so much that I've confused myself."

"Just tell me what you can remember," I urged.

"The orders were for a large pepperoni, two medium plain pizzas, and a large anchovy. But how am I going to match them up with the people who ordered them? I know I took the call from Mr. Burks, but I can't remember what he ordered, so that's no help."

"Well, it's something," I said doubtfully, "but you must remember something else."

"Dad must have taken the order for the two plain pizzas." Danny was beginning to look dejected again.

Vocabulary

dejected: discouraged

Pizza Puzzle   **51**

"You said you took two calls," I reminded him. "Can't you remember anything about the other order?"

"Yes," Danny said. "I spoke to a woman."

"But you don't know what she ordered?"

"No, except that I'm sure it wasn't the anchovies."

"That should do it," I said, grinning at Danny. "Just give me a minute."

I drew a chart below the notes I had taken. The page in my notebook now said:

1. Danny took the order from Mr. Burks.

2. Danny's dad took an order for two plain pizzas.

3. Danny spoke to the only woman who called, and she did not order anchovies.

	Plain	Pepperoni	Anchovy
MR. HARRIS			
MRS. ADLER			
MR. BURKS			

I filled in the chart with Xs and Os, so that in a few seconds it looked like a game of tic-tac-toe. And Danny was the winner. I had matched up a pizza order with each name.

[Can you sort out the orders before you read Ellen's solution on the next page?]

	Plain	Pepperoni	Anchovy
MR. HARRIS	O	X	X
MRS. ADLER	X	O	X
MR. BURKS	X	X	O

"How did you do that?" Danny asked.

"You were sure Mrs. Adler didn't order the anchovy. And, since you took her call but didn't take the call for the plain pizzas, she had to have ordered the pepperoni. That meant Mr. Burks couldn't have ordered the pepperoni. You did take his order, but not the order for plain pizzas, so Mr. Burks ordered the anchovy. And that leaves the plain pizzas as the Harris order."

"Thanks a million!" Danny said. "I have to get these delivered before they get any colder."

1. Why do you think Ellen helps Danny?

____

____

2. How does Ellen solve the pizza puzzle?

____

____

3. Do you think Ellen is used to solving puzzles? Support your answer with evidence from the story.

____

____

4. Describe the type of skills Ellen needs to solve problems like the one in "Pizza Puzzle."

____

____

____

____

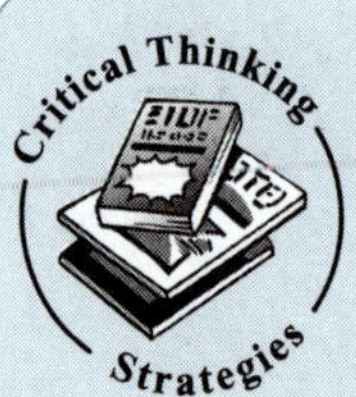

Drawing Conclusions
- First, think about what the text tells you about the topic.
- Next, search for clues in the text that will help you make a logical guess.
- Make connections between the facts and ideas in the text and your own knowledge about the topic.

B Reading   *Making Connections*

**In "Pizza Puzzle," Ellen solves a puzzle using logic.
Develop your own logic skills by finding and completing
similar puzzles. Follow these steps.**

1. Ask your school or public librarian for help locating books of logic or "solve-it-yourself" mysteries.

2. Read at least **two** of the texts you have found and try to solve their puzzles. Assess your ability to solve logic puzzles.

3. Read **two** more texts. Reassess your ability to solve logic puzzles.

4. Continue to read texts and assess your ability to solve logic puzzles. Do you notice any improvement in your ability to solve this type of puzzle? Do you think your ability to solve logic puzzles can be improved? Explain.

____

____

C Language Conventions   *Proper Nouns*

- A **proper noun** refers to a specific person, place, or thing. Proper nouns always begin with capital letters.
    EXAMPLES: Jackie Vivelo writes solve-it-yourself mysteries.

Underline each noun in the sentences below. Circle the proper nouns.

1. Danny Dinello delivers pizza for his dad.

2. I'm sure that Mr. Burks ordered a pizza with anchovies.

3. Did Mr. Harris order two plain pizzas?

4. Mrs. Adler likes pepperoni on her pizza.

5. Without Ellen Sloan's help, Danny wouldn't have solved the pizza puzzle.

Before Reading

Being able to tell what other people are thinking or feeling is really a type of intelligence. Some people are very good at this and other people need practice. Try this quiz and find out how good you are.

Can You Read Minds?

Quiz by Laura Allen

Body language can sometimes give you clues about what others are thinking or feeling. Look at the illustration. Write the letter of each classmate next to what he or she appears to be thinking.

_____ 1. "Is it my turn yet? I'm so nervous."

_____ 2. "Whatever."

_____ 3. "Wow! That's cool."

_____ 4. "I'm grumpy. When's lunch?"

_____ 5. "I can't wait to go to the party tonight."

_____ 6. "Huh? I don't get it."

Answers:
1. c 2. f 3. d 4. b 5. a 6. e

Goals at a Glance

thinking about intelligence • examining images

A   **Critical Thinking**   *Thinking About Intelligence*

1. Being able to tell how people are feeling or what they are thinking by looking at their face and body language is a type of intelligence called **interpersonal intelligence**.

   Some people are really good at this. Others need practice. Record your score from the quiz on page 56.

   ____

2. If you got a perfect score, congratulations! Suggest **one** way this intelligence or skill can help you in your schoolwork or at home.

   ____

   ____

   ____

3. If you didn't do so well on this quiz, you'll want to practise. Look through magazines for photos of people. Try to guess how these people are feeling or what they're thinking.

   Ask someone who got a perfect score on the quiz to look at these photos too. Compare your answers. Is your interpersonal intelligence improving? Explain.

   ____

   ____

   ____

 4. On a scale from **one** to **ten** (one is the least and ten is the most), how do you rank your interpersonal intelligence? Give reasons for your answer.

   ____

   ____

   ____

B Language Conventions   *Adjectives*

> - An **adjective** is a word that describes a **noun**.
>   EXAMPLE: Carmen was in a grumpy mood.
>
> - Adjectives help to create pictures in the reader's mind.
>   Use specific adjectives to give your reader a clear picture.
>   EXAMPLE: Sheila was in a happy mood yesterday.

1. With a partner, create a list of adjectives that could describe a person's mood. Write the list in your notebook.

2. Choose **three** adjectives from your list. In your notebook, write **three** sentences about yourself.

C Visual Communication   *Examining Images*

Work on this activity with at least three classmates. Make sure you talk about the images with each other. Reach an agreement before putting an image into a category.

1. Look through old magazines and newspapers to find images (photos or drawings) of people to match the following moods. Try to find images that show just **one** person.

   angry   happy   sad
   nervous   puzzled   excited

2. Cut out the images and sort them into the above categories. Add labels to these images.

3. Look through more magazines to find **three** more images to add to each category. Make sure you include both males and females, young and old.

4. Did you find it easier to identify the mood of people your own age? People of the same gender? Explain.

____

____

____

Extending: Use the images in **one** category to create a collage or poster.

1. In "Can You Read Minds?" the author has used both text and images to express people's moods. Read over the text and look at this image from page 56.

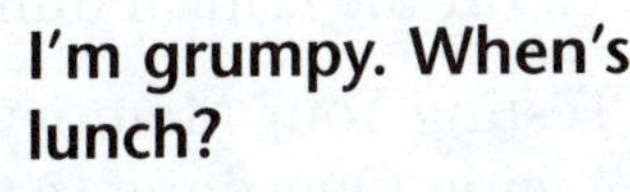

2. Choose **three** images that you found for activity C. Make sure you choose images that show people in **three** different moods.

3. For each image, write **one** sentence that expresses the person's mood. Try to use specific adjectives.

   a. ____

   ____

   b. ____

   ____

   c. ____

   ____

4. Ask a partner to edit and proofread your sentences.

5. On a piece of paper, create a thought bubble (see below) for each of the **six** images on page 56. Neatly print your sentence for each image within a bubble. The bubble should express what the person is thinking. Glue or tape each thought bubble to each image.

Thought Bubble

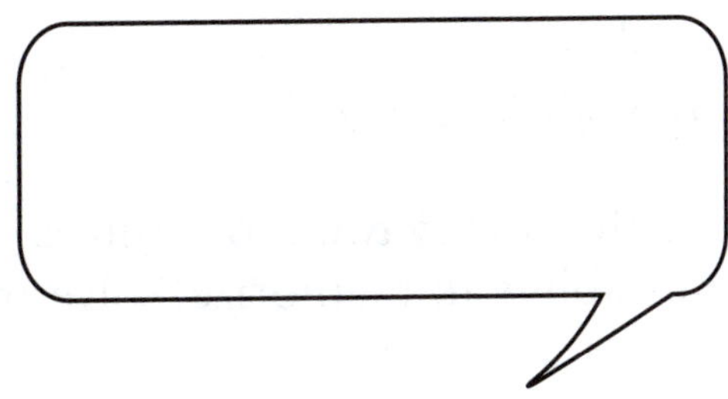

6. Share your images and thought bubbles in a small group. Ask for feedback on the following:
   - your use of specific adjectives
   - how well you express the mood of the person in the image

UNIT 2 WRAP-UP

1. Check off the critical thinking activities you completed during this unit:

   - ❏ Testing Your Memory (page 35)
   - ❏ Asking Questions (page 42)
   - ❏ Responding Personally (page 47)
   - ❏ Drawing Conclusions (page 54)
   - ❏ Thinking About Intelligence (page 57)

2. Describe **one** strategy that helped you complete **one** of these activities.

____

____

Project Idea   *Brain Power Survey*

Step 1. Think about the selections you read in this unit and what you learned about your brain.

Step 2. Complete this survey to assess your ability to memorize, solve puzzles, and read body language.

	Yes	No
1. I eat foods that are good for my brain.	❏	❏
2. I can easily memorize a list of five items.	❏	❏
3. I can easily memorize a list of ten items.	❏	❏
4. I use different techniques to help me memorize.	❏	❏

5. Two techniques that I use are ______________________________

____ .

6. I am good at solving puzzles.	❏	❏
7. I don't understand most body language.	❏	❏

Step 3. During the year, complete the survey **two** more times. Assess whether or not your ability to memorize, solve puzzles, and read body language has improved.

What should you do when you are asked to respond personally to a selection? Below is one student's response to the selection "Fear."

Make Personal Connections

Think about how the selection reminds you of your own life.

"I'm afraid of walking over that bridge. Is that a phobia? How does this phobia affect my life?"

Question Ideas

Question the writer's ideas. Think about your own opinion or ideas on the topic.

"I agree; those are pretty scary things."

Your Response

Think about your response to the selection. Think about why you responded this way to the text.

"I really know how this author feels. Just reading this makes me feel the same way."

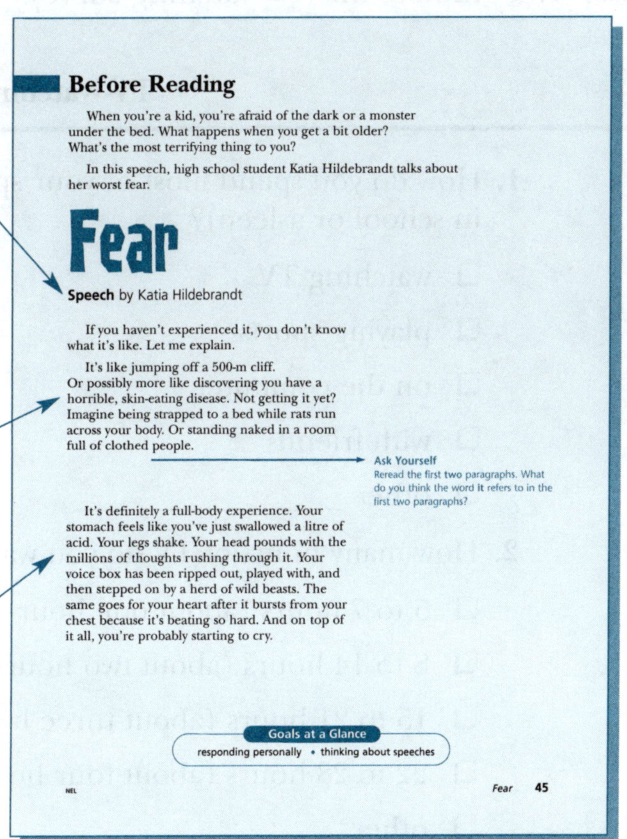

Before Reading

When you're a kid, you're afraid of the dark or a monster under the bed. What happens when you get a bit older? What's the most terrifying thing to you?

In this speech, high school student Katia Hildebrandt talks about her worst fear.

Fear

Speech by Katia Hildebrandt

If you haven't experienced it, you don't know what it's like. Let me explain.

It's like jumping off a 500-m cliff. Or possibly more like discovering you have a horrible, skin-eating disease. Not getting it yet? Imagine being strapped to a bed while rats run across your body. Or standing naked in a room full of clothed people.

Ask Yourself
Reread the first two paragraphs. What do you think the word It refers to in the first two paragraphs?

It's definitely a full-body experience. Your stomach feels like you've just swallowed a litre of acid. Your legs shake. Your head pounds with the millions of thoughts rushing through it. Your voice box has been ripped out, played with, and then stepped on by a herd of wild beasts. The same goes for your heart after it bursts from your chest because it's beating so hard. And on top of it all, you're probably starting to cry.

Goals at a Glance
responding personally • thinking about speeches

NEL   *Fear* **45**

Before Reading
"What Are Canadian Kids Watching?"

Step 1. Complete this TV-watching survey.

TV-Watching Survey

1. How do you spend most of your spare time (when you're not in school or asleep)?
   - ❏ watching TV
   - ❏ playing sports
   - ❏ on the computer
   - ❏ with friends
   - ❏ other _______________

2. How many hours of TV do you watch a week?
   - ❏ 5 to 7 hours (about one hour a day)
   - ❏ 8 to 14 hours (about two hours a day)
   - ❏ 15 to 21 hours (about three hours a day)
   - ❏ 22 to 28 hours (about four hours a day)
   - ❏ other _______________

3. When you watch kids shows, what do you like to watch?
   - ❏ entertainment shows   ❏ education shows   ❏ both

4. What is your favourite TV show? Explain why you like it.

   ____

   ____

   ____

Step 2. Compare your answers with a classmate's answers.

Step 3. Discuss your favourite TV shows.

Read the following TV show profiles. Look at the images. Put a **check mark** (✓) beside any TV show you have watched or would like to watch. Put an **X** beside any TV show you don't want to watch.

What Are Canadian Kids Watching?

TV Show Profiles from CBC, APTN, and YTV

Spy Net on CBC

Spy Net follows the adventures of a spy, code-named Sam, as she carries out her top-secret missions. *Spy Net* reveals real-life spy techniques. Watch *Spy Net* to find out if you have what it takes to become a spy!

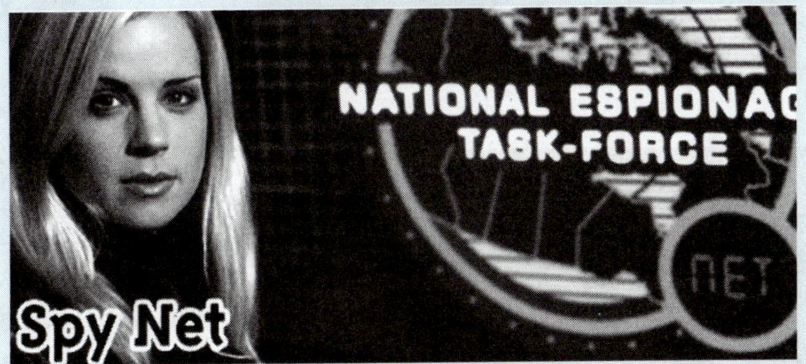

Ace Lightning on CBC

It's not every day a teenager is asked by a superhero to help save the world. Especially when that superhero has come to life out of a video game.

Goals at a Glance

thinking about audience and purpose • comparing TV shows

CG Kids on APTN

Idil Mussa and Sid Bobb are the warm, wacky, talented, and adventurous young hosts of this information-packed *Canadian Geographic* adventure show. The show explores different parts of Canada, as the hosts hang out with local kids. The hosts discover that Canada is an amazing and challenging country. Canada's kids are the coolest, whether living in a condo in downtown Montréal, on a farm in Saskatchewan, or on a boat off the coast of Newfoundland and Labrador!

Longhouse Tales on APTN

Hector Longhouse, played by the actor Tom Jackson, pays for his keep at Tyconderoga's trading post by telling stories about his fun and curious animal friends. This visually stunning show features puppets, exciting live action, and computer graphics. Based on Aboriginal characters and myths, these fast-paced stories are filled with music, laughter, and folklore.

Mystery Hunters on YTV

A true mystery hunter never takes anything at face value! Meet Araya and Christina, true mystery hunters who search for answers to some of the greatest mysteries on Earth…and beyond. There's also Doubting Dave, the magician who shows you how to create your own mysteries. Also on *Mystery Hunters*, discover the truth behind local legends and UFO photos. Are they hoaxes or mysteries?

What Are Canadian Kids Watching?   **65**

Check out your local TV guide to find out what kinds of shows are scheduled before school starts, during the day, after school, and after supper. Look at the schedules for at least **three** different channels. Fill in the chart below.

Times	Types of Shows
Before School	
During the Day	
After School	
After Supper	

Can you draw any conclusions about the types of **audiences** (children, teenagers, adults) that would be watching TV during these times? Explain.

____

____

____

Background Information

- Most TV shows have a very specific **audience** (for example, kids between 9 to 12 who like comic books and adventures).

- Every TV show also has a purpose. The show's **purpose** may be to give information or to entertain.

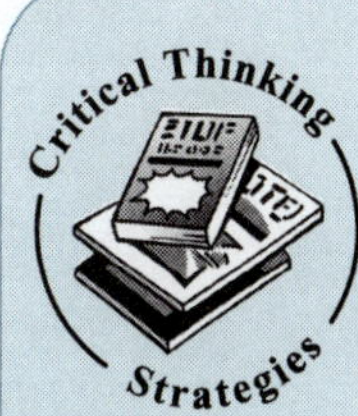

Thinking About Audience and Purpose
- The show's title may give you clues about its audience and the purpose.
- Words that describe a TV show (such as **animated**, **reality show**, or **adventure**) also give you clues about the purpose.
- Commercials during a TV show give you clues about the audience. For example, during a TV show for kids, the commercials may be for toys.

1. a. Choose **one** TV show from "What Are Canadian Kids Watching?"

b. (Circle) some of the following words that you think describe the show.

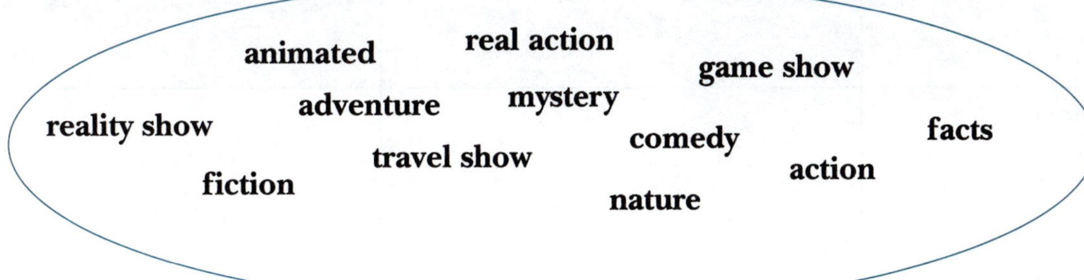

c. Add other words that you think describe this TV show.

2. In the chart below, describe the **purpose** and **audience** for the show you chose.

Show	
Purpose	
Audience	

3. Think about why being able to work out the audience and purpose of that TV show is important.

1. With a partner, discuss some of the TV shows you often watch.

2. Choose **two** TV shows to watch this week. Try to choose shows with different audiences and purposes. Working alone, complete the following chart with information for each show.

Category	TV Show 1 Title: _______________	TV Show 2 Title: _______________
Audience		
Purpose		
Words to Describe the Show		
Your Response (like it or dislike it) and Why		

3. Use the chart to help you compare the **two** TV shows. In your notebook, write a paragraph comparing the TV shows.

Extending: Develop an idea for a show that you would like to see on TV. Use the TV show profiles on pages 63 to 65 as models for a paragraph about your show.

Writer's Craft   *Elaborate Descriptions*

- Some of the TV show profiles use very detailed or **elaborate descriptions** to make the shows seem more exciting.

  EXAMPLE: This visually stunning show features puppets, exciting live action, and computer graphics.

1. Reread "What Are Canadian Kids Watching?" Underline one more example of elaborate description.

2. Put an **E** beside the profiles that use elaborate descriptions. Put an **S** beside any profile that uses simpler descriptions.

3. Choose **one** of the following tasks:

   ❑ Choose a profile that you marked with an **E**. Rewrite it using simpler descriptions.

   ❑ Choose a profile that you marked with an **S**. Rewrite it using more elaborate descriptions.

Extending: Revise the paragraph you wrote in the extending activity for B. Try to add some elaborate descriptions.

- Don't overuse elaborate description in your writing.
- Make sure that your sentences remain clear.

What Are Canadian Kids Watching?

Before Reading
"IMAX: Speed, Power, and Discovery!"

Step 1. Read each statement in the first column.

Step 2. Decide whether the statement is **true** or **false**.
Put a check mark (✓) in that column.

Statement	True	False
IMAX technology was invented in the United States.		
IMAX movies use larger film than normal, as well as larger projection screens.		
IMAX films and screens can show a life-size whale.		
IMAX® Dome uses a dome-shaped screen, surround sound, **and** a scent machine.		

Step 3. With a small group, discuss your answers.

During Reading

As you read, check that you've marked the true or false statements correctly. If necessary, use another coloured pen to change your answer.

IMAX: Speed, Power, and Discovery!

Nonfiction Article by Bev Spencer

Mammoth Scenes

The speeding image is so big it seems to surround you. It is so sharp you feel you could put out a hand and touch it. You feel like you are speeding through the air. The land rushes toward you and tilts.

The scene changes. You are watching the launch of the NASA Space Shuttle. The Shuttle's powerful engine trails flames that seem close enough to fry your face!

The scene changes again. You are far beneath the ocean, walking the sunken halls of the *Titanic*, lost in an <u>eerie</u> gloom.

Nothing has prepared you for the sensations of speed, power, and discovery delivered in these movies. If the movies are this vivid, this awesome, they're probably IMAX. How big are IMAX films? They can be as high as an eight-storey building!

An astronaut is at work in the IMAX movie *Destiny in Space*.

Vocabulary

eerie: spooky

Goals at a Glance

drawing conclusions • brainstorming movie ideas

Inventing Maximum Visual Impact!

The idea for IMAX came from a show called *Labyrinth*, which used several screens and projectors to project one film. This show was created for the 1967 World Exposition in Montréal. In this show, viewers received ten times the information they usually got from a film.

Engineers and filmmakers from Toronto, Ontario, produced the first IMAX film using a larger-than-normal camera and 70-mm film (the largest film frame in history) to produce crisp, brilliant, giant images. Six million people saw this film at Japan's World Exposition in 1970.

An Australian named Ron Jones had invented a special projector that could handle larger film. The IMAX inventors made some changes to this projector to help them solve the technical problems of the oversized film.

The first permanent IMAX theatre, called Cinesphere, opened at Ontario Place in 1971. Audiences were fascinated by IMAX's visually stunning shows.

IMAX® Dome

In 1990, a fish-eye lens was put on the camera and projector, so the film could be projected onto an enormous, domed screen, 24 m wide. This created the IMAX® Dome system, which surrounds you in the film experience so you seem to be part of the action. **Surround sound** (speakers on all sides) helps increase the feeling that you are part of the action.

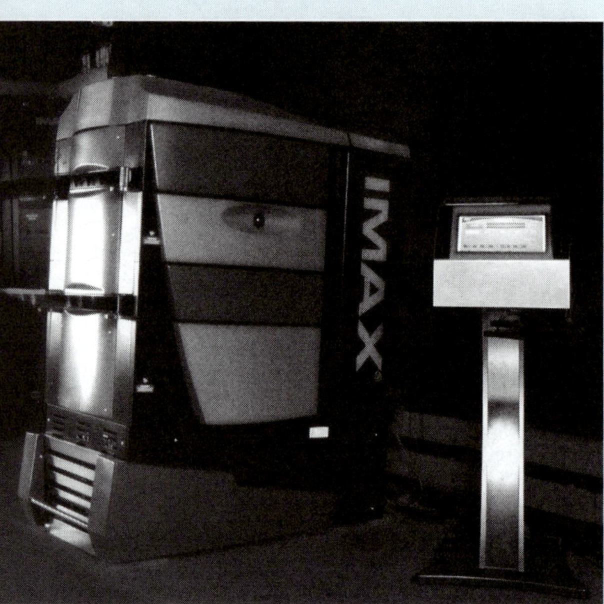

This projector uses 70-mm film.

Vocabulary

fish-eye lens: a wide-angle camera lens that captures a 180° view and is used to produce a circular image

IMAX Today

Today, there are more than 245 permanent IMAX theatres in 36 countries around the world. The screens are made of stretched vinyl and weigh 360 kg. The film itself can weigh 90 kg! Each frame of an IMAX film is 70 mm by 70 mm, ten times larger than the usual 35-mm film. A 45-minute movie uses 5 km of film!

IMAX screens can show a life-size whale (20 m high by 27 m wide). Getting these huge images on film is not easy. A large camera, weighing 39 kg with lens and film, is used. But many of the subjects have been worth the trouble, like the Space Shuttle, the sunken *Titanic*, and some spectacular coral reefs, mountains, and canyons. IMAX films can take people places they have only dreamed of going.

Media Detective!

Step 1. An IMAX film frame is 70 mm by 70 mm. On a blank piece of paper, draw a square to represent the size of IMAX film.

Step 2. A regular movie film frame is 35 mm across and 22 mm long. Within your first square, draw a rectangle to represent the size of regular movie film.

Step 3. Think about the differences in size and shape. Think about the problems the first IMAX inventors and directors had to overcome.

Step 4. What shape of screen would be best to show a regular film on? What shape of screen would be best to show an IMAX film on?

IMAX: Speed, Power, and Discovery! **73**

1. Why is creating an IMAX film so difficult?

2. What have been some of the topics of IMAX films?

B **Critical Thinking** *Drawing Conclusions*

1. What advantages does an IMAX film have over a regular film?

2. What disadvantages does an IMAX film have that a regular film doesn't have?

3. Use the information in the selection to compare IMAX films and regular films.

Media *Brainstorming Movie Ideas*

1. With a small group, **brainstorm** possible topics for an IMAX film. (Remember how an IMAX film is different from a regular film.)

2. Talk about each idea. Together, choose the best idea.

3. Write a short paragraph explaining why your idea would make a good IMAX film. Include a note about your audience and purpose. (Use the TV show profiles on pages 63 to 65 as models.)

> When you **brainstorm**, everyone gives his or her ideas on one topic. Write down every idea. Listen carefully, because other people's words will trigger your own ideas.

Vocabulary *Metric Terms*

- **Metric** is a system of **measurement** based on tens. Here is a list of the most common metric measurements that measure length, mass, and volume:

Length	Mass	Volume
millimetre	milligram	millilitre
centimetre	centigram	centilitre
metre	gram	litre
kilometre	kilogram	kilolitre

- When you're reading metric measurements, look at the prefix (**milli, centi,** and **kilo**) to help you figure out the length, mass, or volume of the object being measured.

- These prefixes are number prefixes. For example, if you look at the prefix **kilo** in **kilometre** you'll know that a kilometre is one thousand metres.

1. <u>Underline</u> the metric measurements in the selection "Imax: Speed, Power, and Discovery!"

2. Write the long forms of the metric measurements you underlined.

_______________________________   _______________________________

_______________________________   _______________________________

IMAX: Speed, Power, and Discovery! **75**

During Reading
"Movie Special Effects"

As you read, (circle) any words that you don't know.

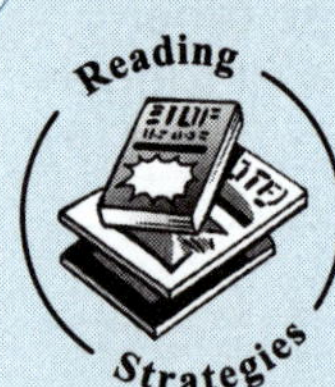

Using Conventions of Text

Use these **text conventions** to help you read the following timeline.

- Timelines give you information about a topic in the order in which events happen. Think about when events happened and the order they happen in.

- Some timelines use arrows to show you the order of events. Read in that order.

- Some timelines have images that help to explain the information. Use the images to help you understand the text.

Vocabulary

interactive: communication between a computer system and the person using it

Movie Special Effects

Timeline and SFX Terms by Nancy Christoffer

1895

The Edison Kinetoscope Company creates the **substitution shot**. In *The Execution of Mary, Queen of Scots*, the camera is shut off after the actor puts her head on the chopping block. A dummy is put on the block and the camera is turned back on.

1916

Frank Williams invents a **matte system**. Moving characters are photographed against a solid background. The characters and the background are then separated and a new background is inserted.

1927

 You ain t heard nothin yet! are the first spoken words on film. Al Jolson in *The Jazz Singer* begins the era of **talkies** (talking films), with these words.

1896

Georges M li s makes a film in which a woman is turned into a skeleton. He uses a technique called **stop-motion photography**.

1925

The Lost World uses stop-motion effects and small **models** to bring over 50 prehistoric animals to life.

1939

The Wizard of Oz uses many special effects. A cyclone is created using a 10.5-m cotton stocking attached to a crane. The model of Dorothy s farmhouse that is sucked up by the cyclone is about 1 m tall.

A scene from the movie *The Lost World* (1925).

Goals at a Glance

supporting examples • investigating movie special effects

1940

Alfred Hitchcock directs *Foreign Correspondent*. He uses **rear projection** to create a dramatic scene of a plane crashing into the ocean.

1961

Ivan Sutherland invents **Sketchpad**. It is the first interactive computer graphics program. An artist uses a light pen to draw diagrams directly on the screen. Very precise diagrams can be created, changed, copied, and stored. Sketchpad makes future inventions in computer animation possible.

1985

The first fully **computer-generated (CG)** character is a knight. It springs to life out of a stained glass window in *Young Sherlock Holmes*. The 30-second sequence takes six months to create.

1956

A huge reptile attacks Tokyo in *Godzilla, King of the Monsters*. Godzilla is really actor Huro Nakjima in a 45-kg costume walking across a model of the city.

1977

Star Wars features complex space battles using electronic **motion control**. These scenes are created from many different images, such as spaceships, star fields, planets, and laser bursts. Computers are used to pull all the images together to create a complete scene.

A scene from the movie
Godzilla, King of the Monsters (1956).

1988

Who Framed Roger Rabbit combines live action with animation. Animated characters, such as Roger Rabbit, share scenes with live action human characters. This kind of computer animation makes the animated characters appear **three-dimensional (3-D)** and lifelike.

1995

Toy Story is the first entirely CG movie. It takes four years to make.

2004

The Polar Express is the first film to be shot entirely in **performance capture**.

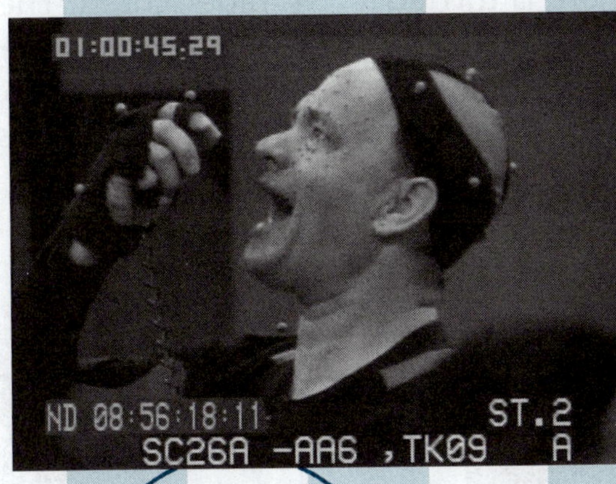

Tom Hanks' movements and facial expressions are used to create a CG character.

1989

James Cameron uses **morphing techniques** in *The Abyss*. Computer-animated water morphs, or changes, into human faces.

1997

The movie *Titanic* uses traditional methods and modern digital methods to create over 450 special effects shots. The ship is a combination of CG effects and a 14-m scale model. The people on deck are often CG characters created with **motion-capture**.

Movie Special Effects   **79**

Special Effects Terms

In **stop-motion photography**, the camera and action is stopped while something is added to or removed from the scene. The camera is turned back on and the action continues. This technique allows objects to disappear and reappear on film. It also allows objects to change into other objects.

This shot from the movie *Voyage to the Moon* was created using stop-motion photography.

The **matte system** is later improved to become **blue-screen photography**. An actor is filmed in front of a plain blue screen. The blue area is later erased from the frame, making the area transparent. The background detail can now show through this blank area.

Helicopters and the actors are filmed in front of a blue screen. A background scene later replaces the blue screen to create a complete scene.

In **rear projection**, a background scene is projected behind actors on a set in a studio. (Rear projection is used instead of shooting on location.) For example, the actors sit in a car that is not moving, while a background of images, such as cars passing, is projected behind them.

In **motion control**, a camera is programmed to precisely copy the same movement over and over again. Many elements can be filmed in exactly the same way. This allows different images to be layered one on top of the other.

Motion-capture is the 3-D animated representation of a live performance. High-speed cameras capture an actor's movements by using reflective body markers. The cameras' reading of the movement of the body markers is sent to a computer. The computer can then make an animated character.

Performance capture is an advanced form of motion-capture. An actor has hundreds of electronic markers attached to his or her body and face. (Think of each marker as a sticky-note.) Each marker sends information about the actor's movements and expressions back to the computer software. This information is then used to create a CG character.

Media Detective!

Research to find out what special effects were used in your favourite movie. Report what you discover to your class.

 **A**   **Critical Thinking**   *Supporting Examples*

Imagine that you are the specials effects person on a movie set before the year 1960. What kind of special effects techniques would you use to create each scene?

1. You're filming a scene that calls for dinosaurs to run across the road.

____

____

2. You're filming a scene in which a small plane crashes into a lake.

____

____

3. You're filming in the studio, but the director wants to film an outdoor scene showing the actors driving down a road in a truck.

____

B   **Vocabulary**   *Developing Definitions*

1. Look at any words you circled as you read the selection.

2. Put a question mark (**?**) beside any words that you couldn't figure out.

3. Write a definition for **one** word that you've put a question mark beside. You may need to use a dictionary.

Word: ____

Definition: ____

____

1. Choose **two** movies you have enjoyed that use special effects.

2. Complete the following chart.

Question	Movie 1 Title: _______________	Movie 2 Title: _______________
What special effects were used in the movie?		
Were the special effects believable?		
What is your opinion of the movie?		

3. Based on the special effects, which movie do you think is better? Explain.

____

____

____

____

Self-Assessment   *Media*

1. Check off the media activities that you completed during this unit:

    ❑ Comparing TV Shows (page 68)
    ❑ Brainstorming Movie Ideas (page 75)
    ❑ Thinking About Special Effects (page 83)

2. Assess the work you did to complete this activity. What did you do well?
    What would you do differently next time?

____

____

Project Idea   *Presenting a Media Production Award*

Step 1. Working alone, complete the following chart.

	Name	**Three Reasons It's My Favourite**
My Favourite TV Show		 • • •
My Favourite Movie		• • •
My Favourite Special Effect		• • •

Step 2. With a small group, compare your charts.

Step 3. As a group, choose **one** TV show or movie that is worthy of an
"Outstanding Media Production" award. You must all agree on one.

Step 4. Choose **one** group member to present your choice to the class.

When watching a TV show, think about its purpose and audience.

Title Clues

Look at the title of the show. Think about the information the title gives you.

- This title mentions mystery. You might guess that the purpose of the show is to solve unexplained events or mysteries.

- The title also mentions hunters. You might guess that someone will go out and try to solve mysteries.

Description Clues

Think about words that have been used to describe this show.

- Producers might describe *Mystery Hunters* as a mystery show. This will help you confirm that its purpose is to explain mysteries.

Commercial Clues

Commercials can also give you clues about the audience of a TV show. For example, a TV show with commercials for toys and video games is meant for kids.

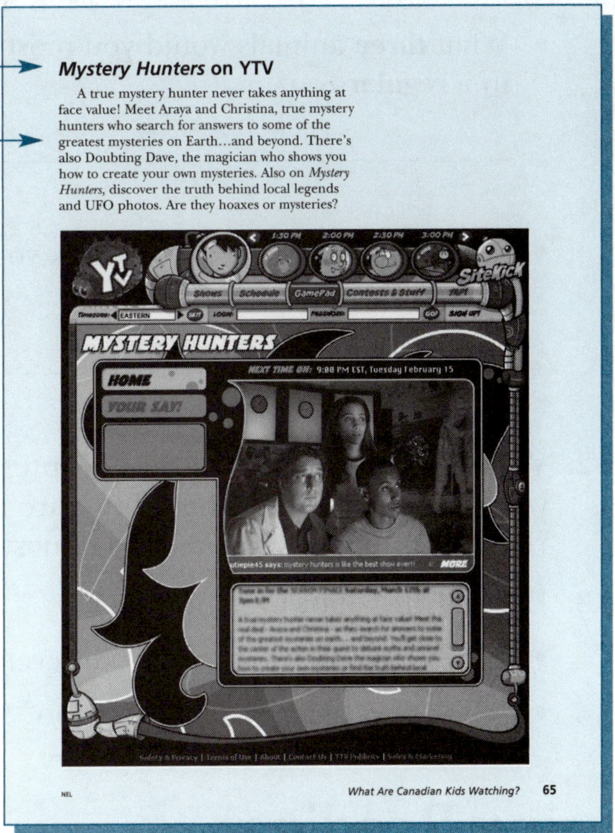

Before Reading
"Tour the Gross Zoo"

Step 1. Work alone to answer the following questions:

- What **three** animals would you most likely find
  in a **regular** zoo?

  ___________________   ___________________   ___________________

- What **three** animals do you think you would
  find in a **gross** zoo?

  ___________________   ___________________   ___________________

Step 2. With a small group, take **five** minutes to discuss
your answers. (Remember, there are no completely
right or wrong answers to these questions.)

Step 3. Discuss the following questions:

- How is a gross zoo probably different from a regular zoo?
- Would you like to visit a gross zoo? Why or why not?

During Reading

As you read each <u>exhibition</u> in the gross zoo,
think about what makes that animal gross.
Based on the information in the selection, give each
exhibition a heading.

Vocabulary

exhibition: a public showing
of something

Tour the Gross Zoo

Article from *Gross Me Out!*
by Sloppy Joe Rhatigan and
Revoltin' Rain Newcomb

Sure we probably look and act gross to a bunch of the animals out there. But here are some animals that are just plain old foul, no matter how you look at them. Come, follow me!

Exhibition #1: One out of every five living things is a beetle.

Exhibition #2: Slime eels are completely covered in the <u>mucus</u> they <u>secrete</u> out of their 90 slime <u>pores</u>. If you get slimed, you have to pull the stuff off. The mucus just gets thicker in water, so it can't be washed off.

When they eat, slime eels slither along the ocean floor until they come across a dead or dying fish. They slither into the animal, through the mouth, eye, or any other opening, and then eat the animal from the inside out.

Scientific Words
Look at the <u>underlined</u> words in the third paragraph. Some of these words you may have heard or seen before. If you don't know what these words mean, look them up in a dictionary.

> **Goals at a Glance**
> making connections • developing a KWL chart

Exhibition #3: There are over 4000 kinds of cockroaches. The world's biggest cockroach is 15 cm long and has a 30-cm wingspan. A cockroach can live a week without its head before it dies of thirst.

Exhibition #4: Leeches are a type of worm that eats blood. Some leeches have three jaws that can clamp on to animals. At one meal, leeches can eat several times their own weight in blood.

Exhibition #5: A toad or frog pushes its eyeballs back in its head to help it swallow.

Exhibition #6: A type of African mongoose has a butt that looks like a flower. As soon as an insect lands on the "flower," the mongoose whips its head around and chomps the bug.

Exhibition #7: A gecko (a type of lizard) can lick its own eyeballs.

A Critical Thinking — *Making Connections*

For the following activity, work with the same small group you worked with in the Before Reading activity on page 86.

1. Now that you've read "Tour the Gross Zoo," discuss these questions again:
   - How is a gross zoo different from a regular zoo?
   - Would you like to visit a gross zoo? Why or why not?

2. What **three** new animals could be added to the gross zoo? Explain why you would add each animal.

3. Compare the headings your group members gave for each exhibition. Choose the best heading for each exhibition.

B Writer's Craft — *Using Informal and Scientific Language*

1. Reread the article. Pay attention to how the authors have used informal language (like **butt**) and scientific language (like **secrete** and **pores**). Circle the informal language. Underline the scientific language.

2. Suggest **one** reason the authors used both informal and scientific language.

____

____

3. Suggest **one** effect using both informal and scientific language has on the audience.

____

____

4. Suggest **one** way you would revise this article to make it suitable for an audience of students younger than yourself.

____

____

Tour the Gross Zoo **89**

Developing a KWL Chart

A **KWL** chart (**K**now, **W**ant to Know, **L**earned) can help you research a topic.

- In the **K** column, list what you already **KNOW** about the topic.
- In the **W** column, think of **three** questions that you **WANT** to find answers for.
- After you have read about your topic, write the answers to your questions in the **L** column.

1. Choose **one** animal from "Tour the Gross Zoo" that interests you. Record what you already know about this animal in the **K** column.

Research Topic	K What I <u>KNOW</u>	W What I <u>WANT</u> to Know	L What I <u>LEARNED</u>
Animal's Name _______			

2. In the **W** column, write at least **three** questions you have about the animal.

3. Think about where you can find answers to your questions. Talk to your teacher about books you can use.

4. Look for answers to your questions. Write the answers in the **L** column.

5. Explain how creating a KWL chart helped you research the animal.

____

____

Before Reading
"What in the World Are Extremophiles?"

Extremophiles are life forms that live in extreme conditions, like boiling water or ice.

Draw a picture of what such a life form might look like. Let your imagination go. Don't worry about being judged on your drawing.

Vocabulary

spring: a stream of water flowing naturally from the earth

organisms: living animals or plants

microscopic: so small that you need a microscope to see

vents: openings in the earth or sea bottom that allow liquids and gas to escape

radiation: radioactive rays that are harmful to living things

What in the World Are Extremophiles?　　**91**

What in the World Are Extremophiles?

Science Article by Pippa Wysong
from "Ask Pippa" in *The Toronto Star*

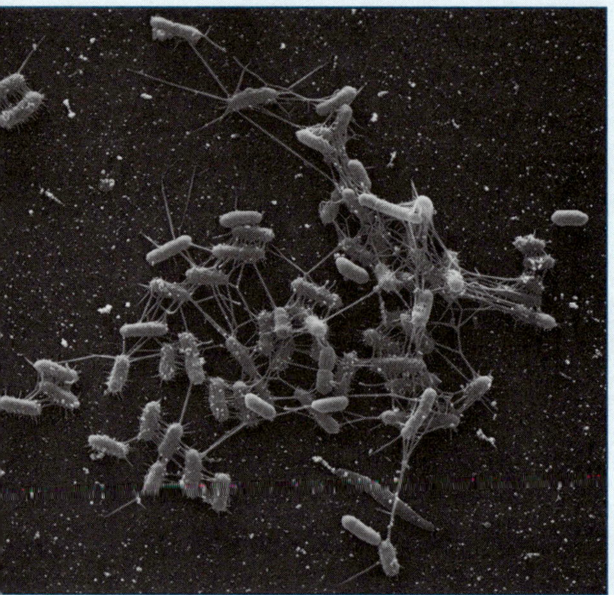

These bacteria live in soil.

If someone told you about something that could live in water that was close to boiling (say in a steamy, smelly hot spring) you might say, "That sounds pretty extreme!" Or, what about something that lives in water that's three times saltier than the ocean? That would be pretty extreme too.

Amazingly, there are life forms that live in extreme conditions, extreme compared to most other conditions on the planet. It makes sense that these life forms are called **extremophiles** (pronounced ex-TREEM-oh-files). The **phile** part of the word is from the Greek language, meaning "to like." So, these organisms like extreme environments or conditions.

Extremophiles are tiny, microscopic life forms. Some are bacteria (one-cell life forms that are found in the soil, water, air, and in other life forms). Others look like bacteria, but are different. These life forms are called archaea (pronounced ark-KAY-uh). Some scientists describe archaea as being like a primitive kind of bacteria. These scientists believe that archaea have lived on Earth long before other life forms appeared.

Goals at a Glance

demonstrating understanding • developing research questions

Some extremophiles live deep in the ocean where there are hot-water vents. The temperatures in these hot-water <u>vents</u> get as high as 110 °C, and the organisms that live there are quite happy with that.

There is another extremophile that lives in Antarctica in the ice. It survives and grows at temperatures either at, or just below, freezing (0 °C). Another type of extremophile lives in soil and can survive high doses of <u>radiation</u> (close to three million times the amount that would kill a human)!

If you take an extremophile out of its environment and put it in an environment you think is normal (like your kitchen table), it would die. Your kitchen table is not extreme enough for it to survive!

From Super Cold to Super Hot
Extreme Oceans and Their Life Forms

Extreme Facts by Philippe Lévesque

Imagine sinking below the surface of the ocean, any ocean. Pretty soon, you'll start to feel the cold; at 1000 m, the sea around you will be pitch black and freezing cold. Without protection (a diving suit or a submarine), you won't survive the cold.

In some parts of the ocean, when you go down far enough, you enter an area filled with light from glowing animals. Underwater volcanoes constantly erupt lava, minerals, and metals. The lava keeps the water hotter than boiling water! Bacteria, shrimp, tubeworms, and eel-like fish are a few of the life forms that live in this extreme environment. These life forms have not changed in millions of years.

Extreme Facts by Philippe Lévesque

"Monster 'glowing' squid stalk the sea!" could have been the newspaper headline in March 2003.

The setting is the Ross Sea in Antarctica. A fishing boat catches a squid that weighs 150 kg! It has tentacles 5 m long!

What these fishers caught is a very rare but dangerous **colossal squid** (a type of large squid). Colossal squid have eyes the size of your head! They have eight arms and two tentacles, lined with hooks and suckers to capture other fish. Colossal squid are very aggressive and move quickly. These squid like to live in very cold water. They live so deep in the ocean (usually at about 800 m) that it's almost totally dark. Colossal squid can glow in the dark, which helps them find other fish.

No one knows how big colossal squid can grow. The one caught in Antarctica was not fully grown.

Comparison by Size

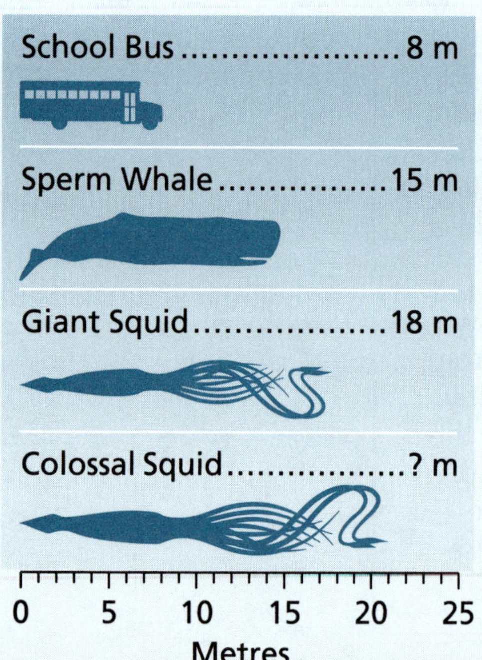

How big are colossal squid? This graph compares the colossal squid to a bus, a sperm whale (one of the biggest mammals on Earth), and the giant squid.

A   Understanding the Selection   *Demonstrating Understanding*

1. Read each statement below. Write **true** or **false** after each statement.

   a. Extremophiles are life forms that like (or live in) extreme environments.

   ____

   b. Extremophiles are very tiny life forms, like bacteria. _________________

   c. Extremophiles can live in any type of environment. _________________

   d. Even deep at the bottom of the ocean, there may be light and warmth.

   ____

   e. Colossal squid have six tentacles and two arms. _________________

2. For the statements you marked **false**, rewrite them so
   that they are true. You may need to reread the selection.

   ____

   ____

B   Vocabulary   *Using Root Words to Work out Meaning*

> - A **root** is a word or part of a word that can help you form other words.
>   EXAMPLE: <u>comfort</u>   <u>comfort</u>able   <u>comfort</u>ably
>   root
>
> - When you read a word that you don't know, see if you can find
>   the root word in it. If you know the root word, you may be able
>   to figure out the meaning of the whole word.

1. <u>Underline</u> the root word of each word below.

   a. fisher   b. saltier   c. usually   d. protection

2. In your notebook, write a definition for each word above.

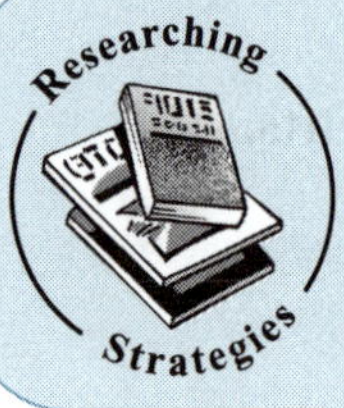

Developing Research Questions
- Think about what you already know about the topic.
- Think about what you want to know.
- Remember the **5 Ws and H** (who, where, why, when, what, and how).

1. Choose **one** of the following topics to research:

- ❏ extremophiles
- ❏ bacteria
- ❏ colossal squid
- ❏ underwater volcanoes
- ❏ tubeworms
- ❏ ocean life

2. List at least **three** questions you have about the topic.

____

____

____

3. Research to find answers to your questions. Write your answers below.

____

____

____

4. Present your research in a fact box like the one on page 93.

Extending: Return to the drawing you created before you read "What in the World Are Extremophiles?" Now that you know more about extremophiles, how would you change that drawing?

Create a drawing for the topic you researched. You can represent that topic realistically or imaginatively.

Before Reading
"All About Bats"

Creating a Concept Web

Creating a **concept web** can help you think about what you already know about a topic.

- First, read the word in the centre circle of the concept web.
- Second, think of another word that is linked to the word in the centre circle. Write the new word in an empty circle.
- Third, think of other words that are linked to the new word. Write the words around the circle you've just filled in.
- Repeat the second and third steps, filling in the web.

Step 1. Complete the following **concept web** with what you know about bats. One branch of the web has been done for you.

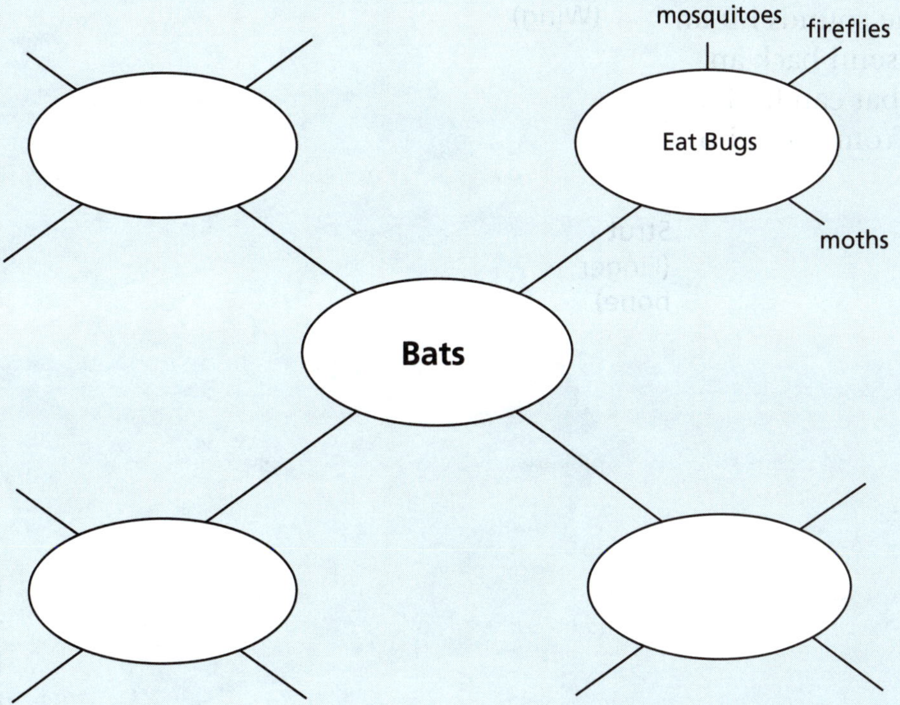

Step 2. With a small group, share your concept webs. Discuss what you already know about bats.

ALL ABOUT BATS

Facts and Diagram from
Creature Features by Anita Ganeri
and Steve Fricker

Bats are strange-looking creatures
with furry bodies and leathery
wings. They sleep during
the day and come out at night
to hunt for juicy moths to
eat. Bats use sound to find
their food. As they fly, they
make very high squeaking
sounds. The sounds hit an
insect and send back an
echo. The bat can find
the insect from the echo.

The bat's leathery wings
stretch between its long,
bony fingers and its legs.

The bat uses its
hooklike thumbs
for climbing,
holding, and
combing its fur.

Goals at a Glance

thinking about learning • using the Internet

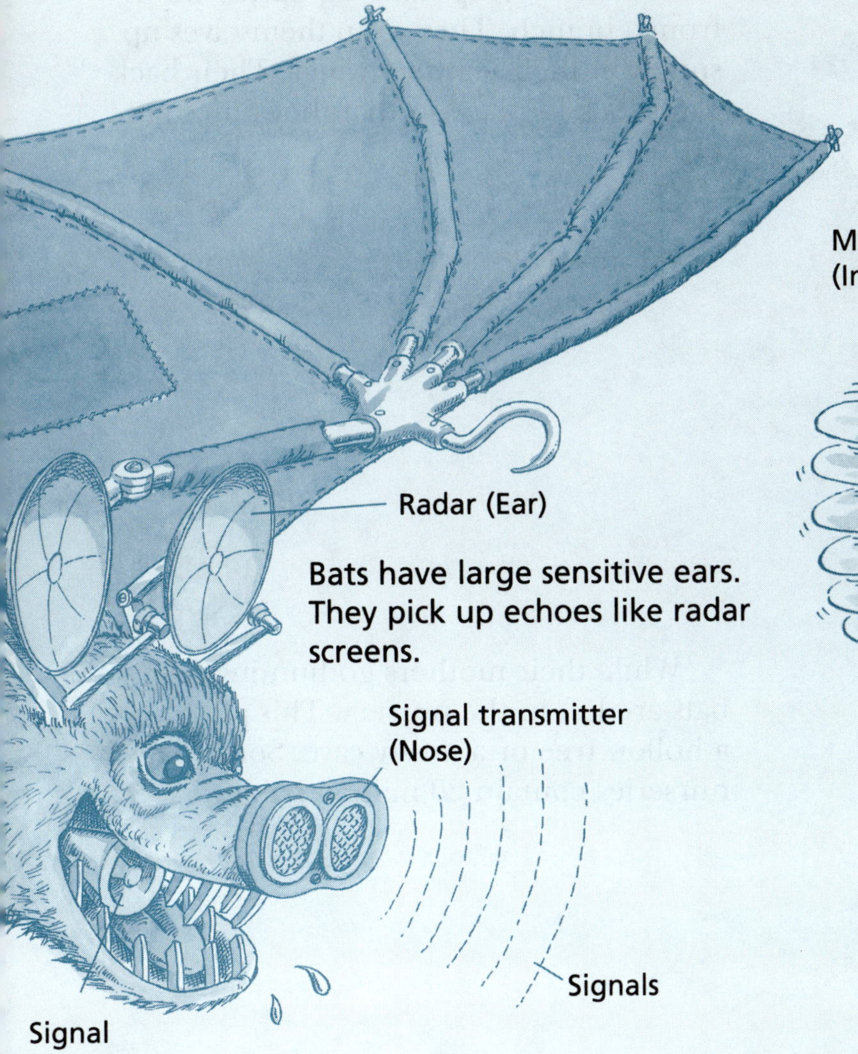

Bats have large sensitive ears. They pick up echoes like radar screens.

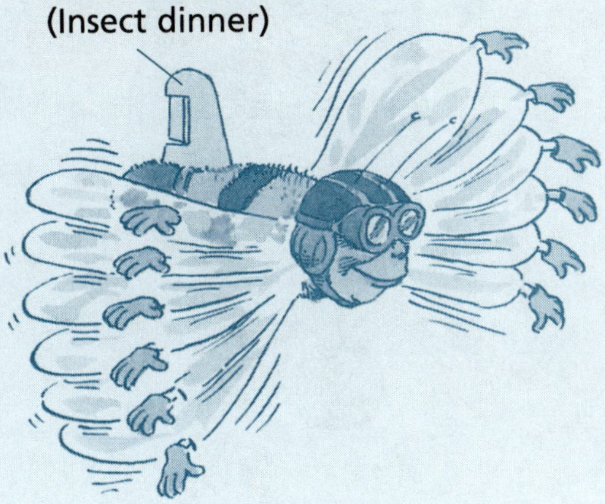

The trick of finding food, such as this busy bee, is called **echolocation**. The bat sends out signals from its mouth or nose that hit the insect, telling the bat where to find its dinner!

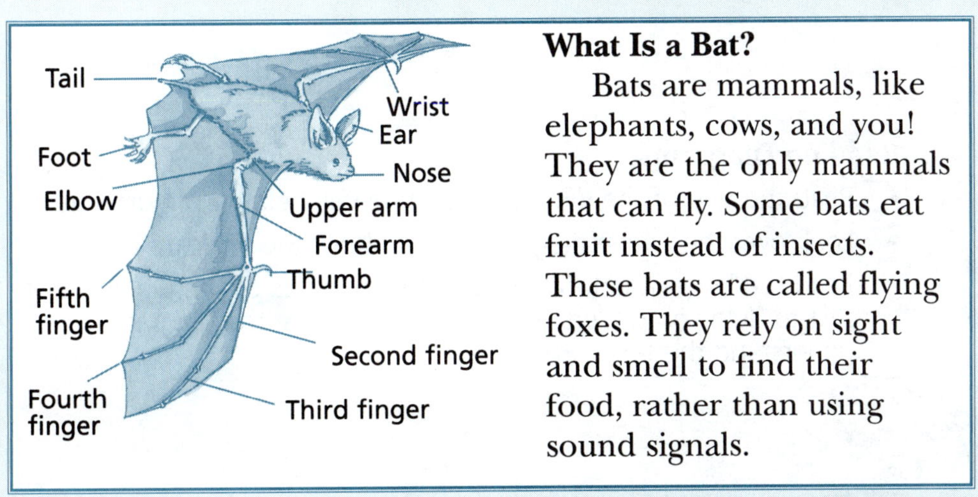

What Is a Bat?

Bats are mammals, like elephants, cows, and you! They are the only mammals that can fly. Some bats eat fruit instead of insects. These bats are called flying foxes. They rely on sight and smell to find their food, rather than using sound signals.

Fruit bats sleep hanging upside down from a branch. They wrap themselves up snugly in their leathery wings. Their back claws lock in place so that they don't fall off!

While their mothers go hunting, baby bats are left in the nursery. This might be a hollow tree or a musty cave. Some bat nurseries contain 20 million babies!

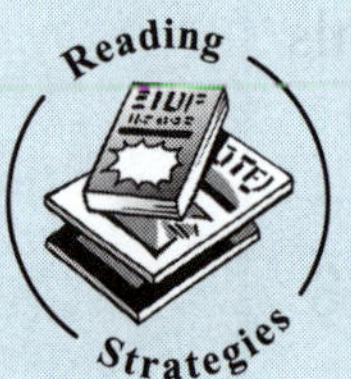

Reading Diagrams

- Read the title of the diagram. The title will help you figure out the topic.
- Look over the whole diagram. Think about the topic.
- Read the labels and look at the different parts of the diagram. Use the text to help you understand the diagram. Use the diagram to help you understand the text.

1. Think about what you learned by reading this selection.

2. Return to the concept web that you completed on page 97. Add any new information to the web. Use a different coloured pen.

3. Read the strategies listed on page 100 for reading diagrams. Use these strategies to help you **reread** the selection and examine the diagram on pages 98 and 99.

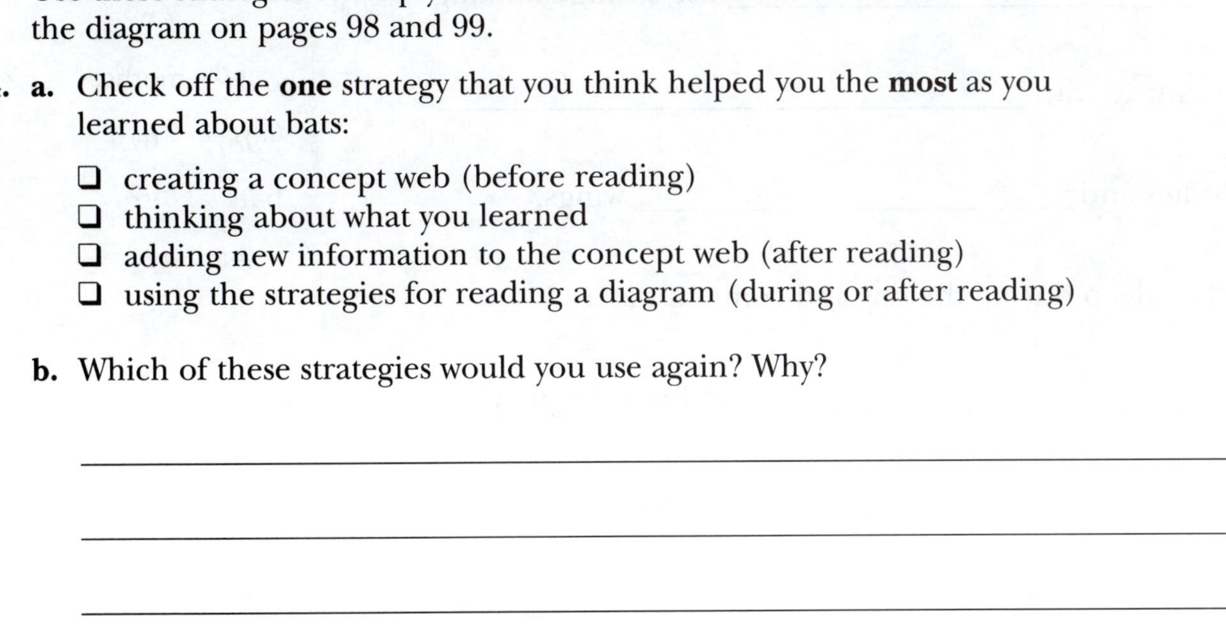

4. **a.** Check off the **one** strategy that you think helped you the **most** as you learned about bats:

    ❏ creating a concept web (before reading)
    ❏ thinking about what you learned
    ❏ adding new information to the concept web (after reading)
    ❏ using the strategies for reading a diagram (during or after reading)

   b. Which of these strategies would you use again? Why?

   ____

   ____

   ____

   ____

1. Complete this paragraph using information
    from "All About Bats." The answer words are
    mixed up in the bat shape.

_______________________________ are strange-looking

creatures with _______________________________

bodies and _______________________________ wings.

They sleep during the day and come out at

_______________________________ to hunt for juicy

_______________________________ to eat. Bats use _______________________________

to find food. As they _______________________________, bats make squeaking sounds.

The sounds hit an insect and send back an _______________________________.

Bats can _______________________________ insects from the echo.

Bats are the only _______________________________ that can fly.

2. Were you able to complete the paragraph? If not, skim the selection
    looking for the words in the bat shape. Reread the sentences where
    those words appear.

3. **a.** Read your completed paragraph to a partner. Ask: Does my
    paragraph sound correct? If not, what answer do I need to change?

    b. Listen as your partner reads his or her completed paragraph to you.
    Let your partner know if the paragraph sounds correct.

C Researching   *Using the Internet*

Read the statements in the box below. Then follow the steps in this activity to find out which statements are <u>true</u> and which are <u>false</u>.

Statements About Bats
True or False?

__________ There are more than 1100 species of bats. _______________________

__________ Bats have been around since the time of
the dinosaurs.   _______________________

__________ The bumblebee bat of Thailand is the
world's smallest mammal.   _______________________

__________ All bats are blind.   _______________________

__________ There are **no** species of bats in Australia. _______________________

__________ Vampire bats suck blood from
large animals, such as cows.   _______________________

1. Decide on the best **key words** to use to research each statement on the Internet. Write your key words in the blank space **after** each statement.

2. Using the Internet, conduct research on bats. The strategies below will help you.

3. When you've finished researching bats, put **T** (for true) or **F** (for false) **before** each statement in the box.

4. For each statement you marked **F**, cross out the part of the statement that makes it false. If necessary, add new information to make that statement true.

Using the Internet
- Use a search engine, such as Google or Yahoo.
- Choose a search word or phrase, such as **vampire bats**.
- Scan the titles on the list that appears. Click on any titles that you think will be useful.

A part of the Atlantic Ocean is called the Bermuda Triangle because of the unexplained events that have happened there. With a partner, discuss what you know about the Bermuda Triangle.

The Mystery of the Bermuda Triangle

Article by Nicole Banks

What Is the Bermuda Triangle?

The sea between Bermuda, Florida, and Puerto Rico is known as the Bermuda Triangle. This area is said to have secret powers that cause ships and planes to disappear. Stories about the area began when five bomber planes vanished after leaving Fort Lauderdale, Florida, on December 5, 1945. The planes were never seen again.

Since 1945, many planes and ships have disappeared in the Bermuda Triangle. To this day, no trace of these ships and planes has ever been found.

Goals at a Glance

forming opinions • developing a report

What Happened to the Ships and Planes?

For the past 50 years, theories to explain the missing ships and planes have included underwater earthquakes, pirates, inexperienced sailors, and pilot error. More recently, Bermuda Triangle experts believe that three theories are the most likely explanations of what happened to the ships and planes:

1. bad weather

2. the Gulf Stream

3. the gas bubble theory

1. Bad Weather

Violent storms build up quickly in the Bermuda Triangle. Many of these storms are not detected by weather-tracking systems. Sometimes, dangerous waterspouts are part of these storms and can destroy any passing ship or plane.

Vocabulary

pilot error: mistakes made by someone flying a plane

waterspouts: spinning funnels of spray and water

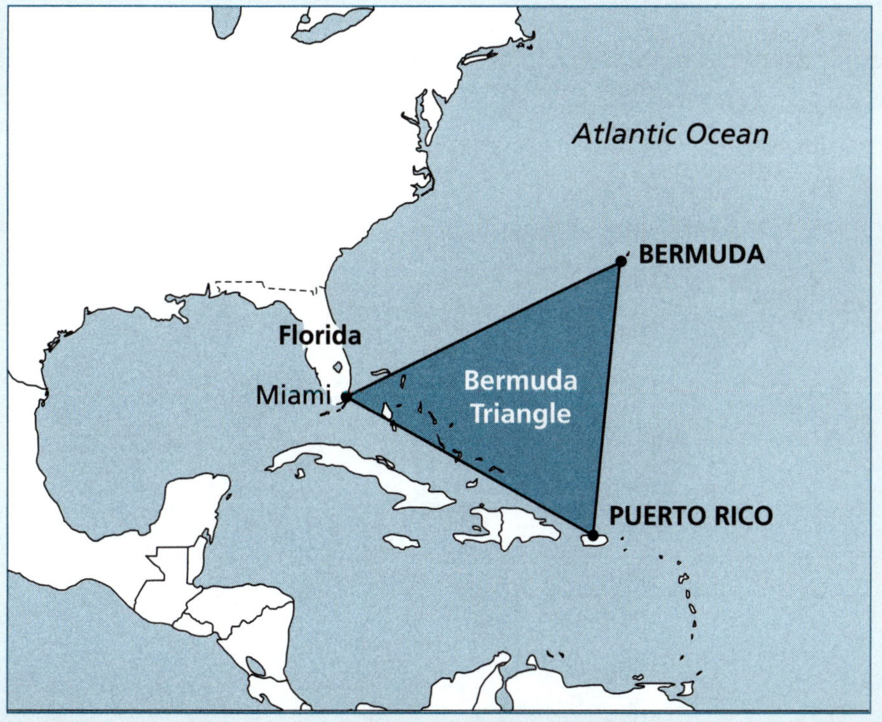

The Bermuda Triangle is in the Atlantic Ocean. The corners of this triangle touch Bermuda, Puerto Rico, and the southern tip of Florida.

2. The Gulf Stream

The **Gulf Stream** is a warm ocean current that runs
through parts of the Atlantic Ocean, east of North America.
The Gulf Stream moves about 8 km/h in some areas.
That's fast enough to throw a ship hundreds of kilometres
off its course if the sailors don't take the current into account
when they navigate.

3. The Gas Bubble Theory

Scientists developed the gas bubble theory.
Large amounts of gas hydrates or gas bubbles in the
area cause the water to become less dense in small
patches. If a ship sails into these patches, it could sink
quickly, without a trace.

Why Is the Mystery Unsolved?

Because the wreckage of these ships and planes has
never been found, investigators cannot tell what has
really happened. Official sources, like the US Navy,
don't believe that there is a Bermuda Triangle.

Famous Planes and Ships Missing in the Bermuda Triangle	
Planes	**Year**
Bomber Flight 19	1945
Martin Mariner	1945
City Belle	1946
Superfortress bomber	1947
Star Tiger	1948
Star Ariel	1949
Flight 441	1954
C-119 Flying Boxcar	1965
Ships	**Year**
USS Cyclops	1918
Revonic	1958
Witchcraft	1967

A Understanding the Selection *Demonstrating Understanding*

1. What is the mystery of the Bermuda Triangle?

2. Why does the mystery of the Bermuda Triangle remain unsolved?

B Critical Thinking *Forming Opinions*

1. **a.** Which explanation for the missing ships and planes do you think is the best?

   b. Why do you think so?

2. Discuss your answers in small groups.

3. If the discussion changed your answers, write your new answers below.

C Researching *Developing a Report*

Choose <u>one</u> of the ships or planes from the fact box on page 106. Investigate the facts behind the disappearance of the ship or plane.

1. Visit your local library and talk to the librarian about books you can use.
2. Search the Internet for Web sites on the Bermuda Triangle and on your chosen ship or plane. Remember to check how accurate and reliable the sites are.
3. Write a paragraph about the events leading to the disappearance of the ship or plane. Use this paragraph planner to plan your paragraph.

Paragraph Planner
Introduction: Write a **topic sentence** that clearly states what your paragraph is about.
Body: Write at least **three sentences** describing what happened.
Conclusion: Write a **concluding sentence** to your paragraph. You might end with a statement about what you believe happened to the ship or plane.

4. Include an illustration or photo of the ship or plane.

Self-Assessment *Researching*

1. Check off the researching activities you completed during this unit:

   ❏ Developing a KWL Chart (page 90)
   ❏ Developing Research Questions (page 96)
   ❏ Using the Internet (page 103)
   ❏ Developing a Report (page 108)

2. In your notebook, complete the following sentences. Describe how your researching skills developed.

   ❏ I'm better at…
   ❏ I now know how to…
   ❏ One important thing about researching that I discovered is…

3. Set **two** goals for using and improving your researching skills in other subject areas.

____

____

Project Idea *Creating a Natural Mysteries Exhibition*

Follow these steps to create a Natural Mysteries Exhibition.

Step 1. Review the selections in this unit. Write down any strange animals or natural mysteries you'd like to include in the exhibition. Choose **one** topic.

Step 2. Create a KWL chart to help you research your topic.

Step 3. Choose the best way to find answers to your questions.

Step 4. Write a fact box for your topic. Include a photo or illustration.

Step 5. With your classmates, create a classroom display of fact boxes for a Natural Mysteries Exhibition.

Before researching a topic it is a good idea to create a KWL chart. A student who wanted to research bats made the KWL chart below.

Topic	K What I **KNOW**	W What I **WANT** to Know	L What I **LEARNED**
Bats	the only mammal that can fly	1. What do bats eat?	1. Some bats eat moths and other insects. Some bats also eat fish, frogs, fruit, or nectar.
	they fly at night; sleep in the day	2. Where do bats live?	2. Bats live almost all over the world (except a few islands).
	over 1000 different kinds of bats	3. How do bats care for their babies?	3. A mother bat uses smell and her baby's cry to recognize her baby. A baby bat drinks its mother's milk until it is ready to fly and hunt alone.

Here are the paragraphs this student wrote using the information from the KWL chart. Compare the paragraphs with the notes on the KWL chart. Notice how all the facts are included in the paragraphs.

Bats are very interesting creatures. Bats are the only mammals that can fly. They fly at night and sleep during the day. There are over 1000 different kinds of bats. They live almost all over the world, except on a few islands.

Although most kinds of bats eat moths and other insects, some bats also eat fish, frogs, fruit, or nectar.

A mother uses smell and her baby's cry to recognize her baby. A baby bat drinks its mother's milk until it is ready to fly and hunt alone.

Before Reading
"Maui and the Great Fish"

This selection is a <u>Maori</u> myth. A **myth** is a story that connects to a people's past and usually tells about some belief about nature. Think about these features of myths as you read "Maui and the Great Fish."

- There is magic.
- The events happen in the past.
- Someone is tested.

Read this introduction by the author of "Maui and the Great Fish."

Note From the Author

This is the story of how <u>Maui</u> caught the Great Fish of New Zealand. When I was very young, I imagined that Maui was very young too and I was very impressed that such a young boy could catch such a great fish.

When I look at my maps of New Zealand, I can see that it is in fact the South Island that is in the shape of a fish. However, I always imagined it was shaped like a shark, not a fish, because when I first heard the story I was terrified of sharks and thought that the shark was the only fish that would fight so violently against Maui's godlike powers.

The Maori name for the North Island is still Te Ika A Maui, meaning the fish-hook of Maui. In other words, Maui used the North Island as his fish-hook to catch the South Island, his Great Fish.

Maui and the Great Fish

Myth from *Land of the Long White Cloud*
by Kiri Te Kanawa

Maui was, they say, half man and half god. He knew many magic spells and had many magic powers that his older brothers didn't know about, or if they did they pretended to ignore.

Once, when he heard his brothers talking about going fishing, Maui decided that he wanted to go too. So, before his brothers had woken up he went down to where the canoe was, carrying his special fishing hook. Hearing his brothers approach, he quickly hid under the floorboards of the boat.

The brothers arrived, and they were laughing about having managed to escape without Maui. They were looking forward to having a good day's fishing without being bothered by their young brother.

They pushed out from shore and were still laughing when suddenly they heard a noise.

"What was that?" asked one of them.

Then they thought they heard someone talking. They couldn't see anyone; they couldn't see anything except for the water.

"Oh, it must have been a seagull or something screeching in the distance," suggested another of the brothers.

Vocabulary

Maori: the Aboriginal people of New Zealand

Maui: a hero of myth for the Maori

Goals at a Glance

retelling the myth • making comparisons

Then they heard the sound again. It was Maui, laughing and saying in a strange voice "I am with you. You haven't tricked me at all."

The brothers were becoming quite scared now. It sounded like muffled speech but there was no one to be seen.

On they paddled into the deep waters. Again they heard the voice and this time one of the brothers said he thought the noise was coming from under the floorboards so he wrenched up a few. There was Maui, laughing loudly and boasting "I tricked you! I tricked you!"

The brothers were amazed to see Maui there. They decided to turn back immediately. "You are not coming with us," they said. "You're far too young and our father doesn't want you to come with us."

But Maui said, "Look back! Look back to the land! Look how far away it is!"

He had used his magic powers to make the land seem much further away than it really was. The brothers, not realizing that it was a trick, reluctantly agreed to take Maui with them.

They paddled on for a while and then stopped. Just as they were about to throw over the anchor and start their fishing, Maui said, "No. Please don't do that because I know a much better place further out, full of fish, all the fish you could want. Just a little while longer and you'll have all your nets filled in half the time."

Vocabulary

reluctantly: unwillingly

Maui and the Great Fish   **113**

The brothers were tempted by this promise of fish and paddled out a little further when Maui stopped them and told them to start fishing. So they threw over their nets which within a few minutes were overflowing. They couldn't believe their luck.

Their boat was lying low in the water with the weight of their catch so the brothers told Maui they were going to turn back. But Maui said, "No, it's my turn. I haven't had a chance to do my fishing."

"But we have enough!" they replied.

"No! I want to do my fishing," insisted Maui.

With that, he pulled out his special fishing hook made of bone, and asked for some bait. The brothers refused to give him any so Maui rubbed his nose so hard that it began to bleed. Then he smeared the hook with his own blood and threw it over the side.

Suddenly the boat was tossed about, and Maui was thrilled because he was sure he had caught a very big fish. He pulled and pulled. The sea was in a <u>turmoil</u> and Maui's brothers sat in stunned silence, marvelling at Maui's magic strength.

Maui heaved and tugged for what seemed like an age until at last the fish broke the surface. Then Maui and his brothers could see that what he had caught was not a fish but a piece of land, and that his hook was <u>embedded</u> in the doorway of the house of Tonganui, the son of the Sea God.

Maui's brothers couldn't believe their eyes. This beautiful land pulled up from the sea was smooth and bright, and there were houses on it and burning fires and birds singing. They had never seen anything so marvellous in their whole lives.

Realizing what he had done Maui said, "I must go and make peace with the gods because I think they are very angry with me. Stay here quietly and calmly, until I return."

As soon as Maui had gone the brothers forgot his instructions and began to argue for possession of the land.

"I want this piece," said one.

"No! I claimed it first. It's mine!" shouted another.

Soon the brothers began to slash at the land with their weapons. This angered the gods even more and its smooth surface was gashed and cut. It could never be smoothed out again.

To this day, those cuts and bruises of long ago can still be seen in the valleys and mountains of New Zealand.

Maui and the Great Fish **115**

Retelling the Myth
- Use your own words when you retell a myth.
- Tell about the most important events and characters.
- Follow the same order as the original myth. Use words like **first**, **then**, **next**, and **after** to show the order of the events in the story.

Follow these steps to retell "Maui and the Great Fish" to a partner.

1. Reread the myth. On each page, make a note about the most important things that happened in that part of the story. For example, on page 112, you might note that Maui sneaks away to go fishing with his brothers.

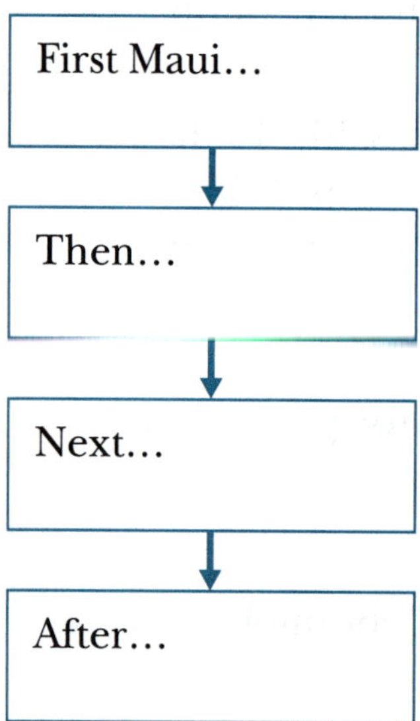

2. Practise telling the myth. Use your notes to help you.

3. Retell the myth to a partner.

4. Listen to your partner retell the myth to you.

5. Did retelling the myth increase your understanding of it? Explain.

____

____

____

B Critical Thinking   *Making Comparisons*

1. Find and read **one** other myth. (Your teacher or librarian can help you find some.)

2. With a partner, discuss the myths you've just read (including "Maui and the Great Fish").

3. Together, review the list of myth features on page 111. Discuss how these myths are the same and how they are different.

4. Create a **Venn diagram** to compare the **two** myths.

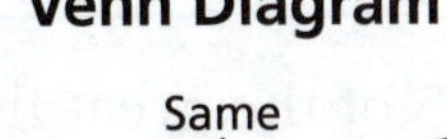

Venn Diagram

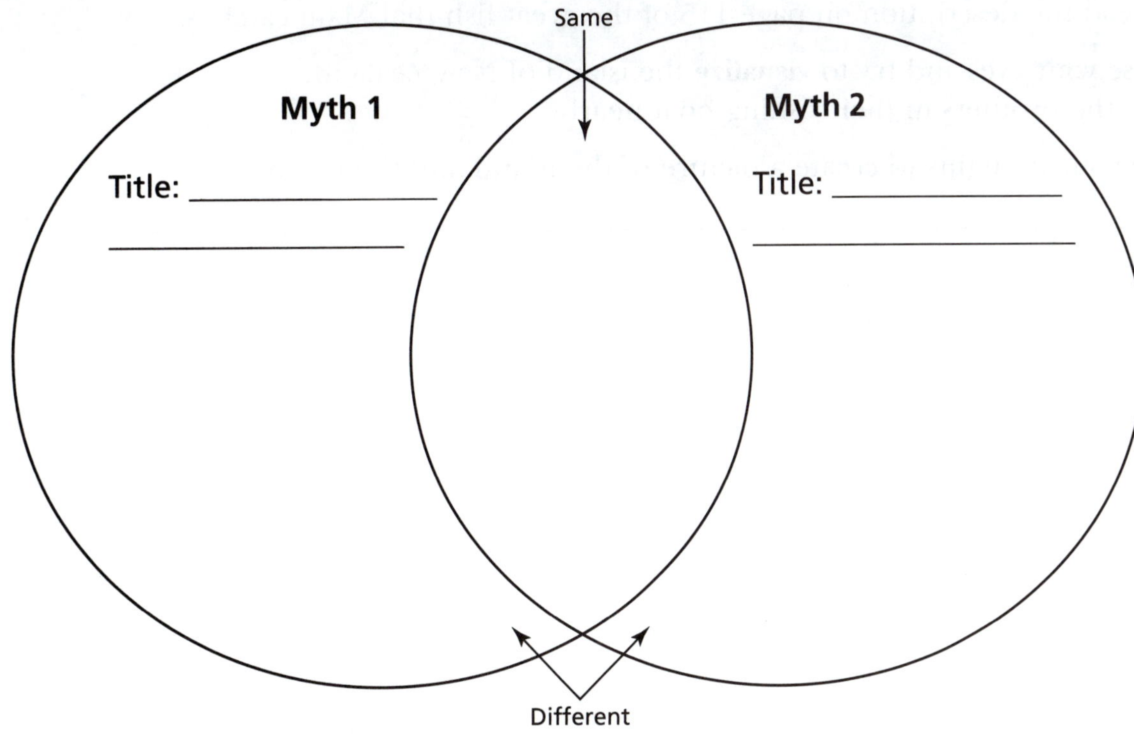

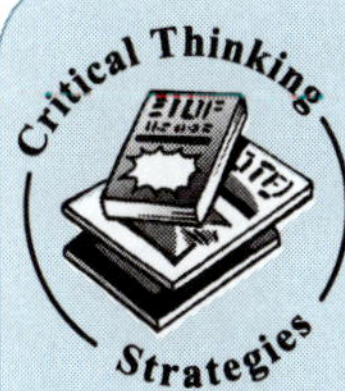

Making Comparisons

A **Venn diagram** is used to compare **two** things. It shows how these two things are the same and how they are different.

- Each thing being compared has its own circle.
- There is a space where the two circles overlap. Write facts about how the two things are the **same** in this space.
- Write facts about how the two things are **different** in the other part of each circle.

Maui and the Great Fish   **117**

- Writers use **description** to help readers **visualize** (picture in their minds) events or settings.

  EXAMPLES: This <u>beautiful</u> land pulled up from the sea was <u>smooth</u> and <u>bright</u>, and there were houses on it and <u>burning</u> fires and birds <u>singing</u>.

- Writers create good descriptions by using many details, descriptive adjectives, and specific nouns and verbs.

1. Reread the description on page 115 of the great fish that Maui catches.

2. Close your eyes and try to **visualize** the island of New Zealand, with the brothers in their fishing boat nearby.

3. Use your thoughts to create a picture of the island and the brothers.

Extending: Look at the picture of the fishing boat on page 114. In your notebook, write a paragraph describing that boat. Remember to use details, descriptive adjectives, and specific nouns and verbs.

Before Reading
"Oak Island Money Pit"

Step 1. Work with a small group to discuss the following situations. Think about what you would do in each situation.

- You find $20 in the school cafeteria. You are all alone and no one is in sight.

- You find a wallet filled with money. The owner's name and phone number are in the wallet.

- You find a map for a treasure buried by pirates hundreds of years before you were born.

Step 2. Now discuss these situations from a **new perspective** (point of view). Again, think about what you would do in each situation.

- You get back to class after lunch and discover you've lost $20. You need that money for a school trip. What will you do if you don't get it back?

- You get to the grocery store and discover you've lost your wallet. Oh no, how will you pay for food this week? Even worse, you're leaving on a trip the next day and now you don't have any ID.

- You own the land on which treasure seekers are digging for treasure. If they find anything, does it belong to you or them?

Vocabulary

coconut fibres: long, threadlike material from the shell of a coconut

parchment: paper made from the skin of a sheep or goat

Oak Island Money Pit

Diagram by Tina Holdcroft

Sixteen-year-old Daniel McGinnis forgets all about hunting when he sees a strange sight. An old ship's pulley, tied to a tree, dangles over a dent in the earth below.

This can only mean one thing. Something heavy was lowered into the ground with the pulley, then buried. Can it be the pirate treasure of Captain Kidd?

Daniel's discovery in 1795 begins a treasure hunt on Nova Scotia's Oak Island that lasts for more than 200 years!

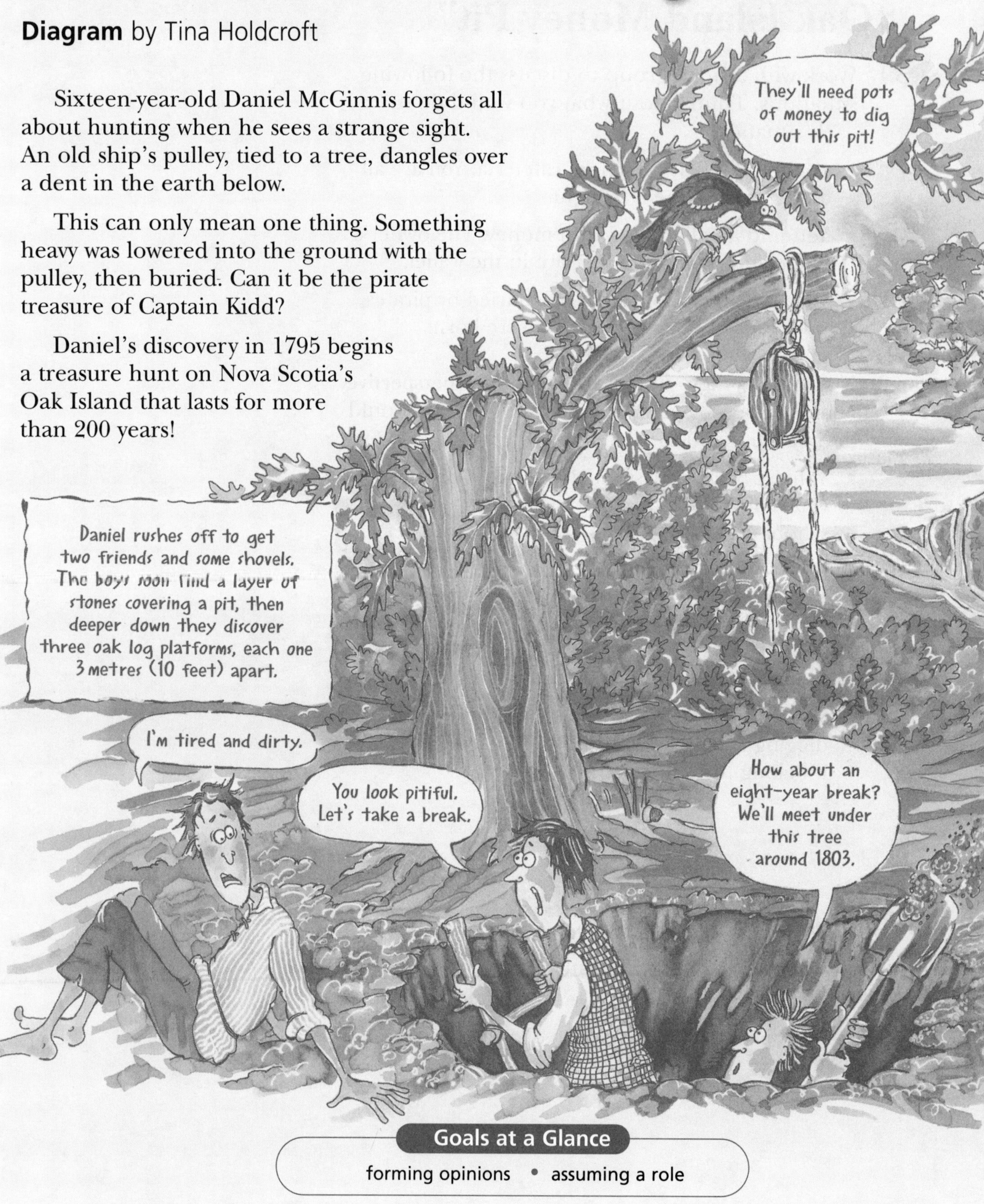

Goals at a Glance

forming opinions • assuming a role

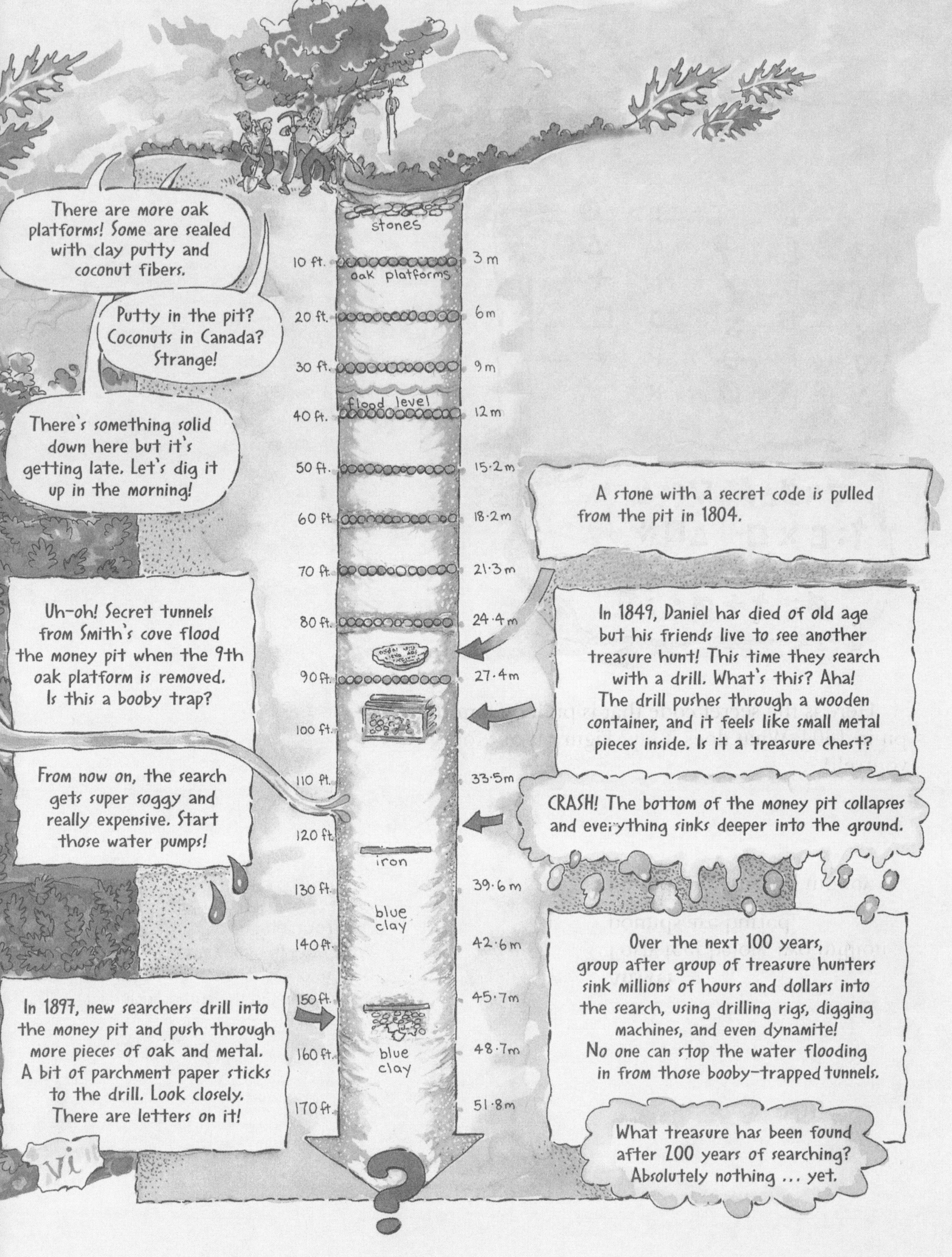

Oak Island Money Pit **121**

Here is the secret code that is pulled from the pit in 1804. What does it say? Figure it out for yourself!

Ask Yourself
What does the question mark at the bottom of the diagram on page 121 mean? Why did the author include it?

Critical Thinking — *Forming Opinions*

**You will <u>not</u> find the answers to these questions in the selection.
There are no right or wrong answers. You need to think about each
question and give your opinion.**

1. Discuss these questions with a small group:

   • Do you believe there really is treasure at the bottom of the
   Oak Island Money Pit? Why or why not?

   • Would **you** spend all your life (as some people have) and all your
   money trying to find a treasure that might not even exist? Why or why not?

   • If the treasure is ever found, who do you think should get it?
   ❏ the people who find it
   ❏ the people who own the land
   ❏ the government of Nova Scotia or Canada
   ❏ the **descendants** (great, great, great-grandchildren) of Captain Kidd
   ❏ the descendants of Daniel McGinnis

2. Think about the discussion you've just had. Choose **one** question and
   write a paragraph in response to that question. Include your opinion
   and the opinions of your group members.

____

____

____

____

____

____

____

____

Extending: Based on the diagram on pages 120 and 121, create a model
of the Oak Island Money Pit. Your model should show a cut-away view of
the tunnel, as the diagram does. Use materials like clay, twigs, straw, and
pebbles. Add labels to the model. Will you put a treasure at the bottom of
the pit?

Oral Communication   *Assuming a Role*

1. Choose **one** of the three situations you discussed in the Before Reading
    activity on page 119:

    - found money/lost money
    - found money/lost wallet
    - found treasure map/own the land

2. Put yourself in the role of **one** of the two people in that situation.
    (That is, either you have lost the money or you have found it.)
    With a partner taking the other role, role-play a conversation
    between these two people.

3. Switch roles with your partner and discuss the situation again.

Writer's Craft   *Interjections*

- An **interjection** is a short statement or exclamation that expresses feeling.
  Many interjections express surprise, sadness, or joy.
  EXAMPLES: Aha! Oh!

- Interjections help the reader understand what the characters might be
  feeling or thinking.

1. a. There are **two** interjections in the selection.
        Find and (circle) both.

    b. Decide what feeling each interjection expresses.
        Write your answers in the margin beside the
        interjections.

2. On page 120, the words each boy might have said,
    after treasure hunting all day, are in speech
    bubbles. Add an interjection to each speech
    bubble.

3. In your notebook, create a new speech bubble to
    show how Daniel felt when he first discovered the
    pulley. Include an interjection.

D **Writing** *In Role*

1. Imagine that you are **one** of the following people:

   ❏ Daniel McGinnis after finding the money pit (but not the treasure)
   ❏ a person who has spent his/her entire life looking for the Oak Island treasure
   ❏ Captain Kidd before he buried the treasure

2. Choose **one** of the following formats. (If you're not sure about the structure or features of that format, talk to your teacher.)

   ❏ diary/ship's log   ❏ letter
   ❏ true story   ❏ want ad
   ❏ comic strip   ❏ blog
   ❏ speech   ❏ your choice _______________

3. In role, as the person you chose, answer the following questions.

4. Write the format you chose, in role as the person you chose.

Before Reading
"On Behalf of Coyotes Everywhere"

An **acceptance speech** is a speech given by someone who has received an award or honour.

Imagine that Wile E. Coyote, from the Roadrunner cartoons, was given an award for his loyal customer support of the ACME Supply Company. With a small group, discuss the following questions:

- What do you think Wile E. will have to say about all the time he's spent trying to catch Roadrunner?

- How do you think the story Wile E. tells will be different from the story the cartoons tell?

During Reading

Think about what you know about Wile E. Coyote from the cartoons. Think about how Wile E. comes across differently in this speech. While you read, complete the following diagram.

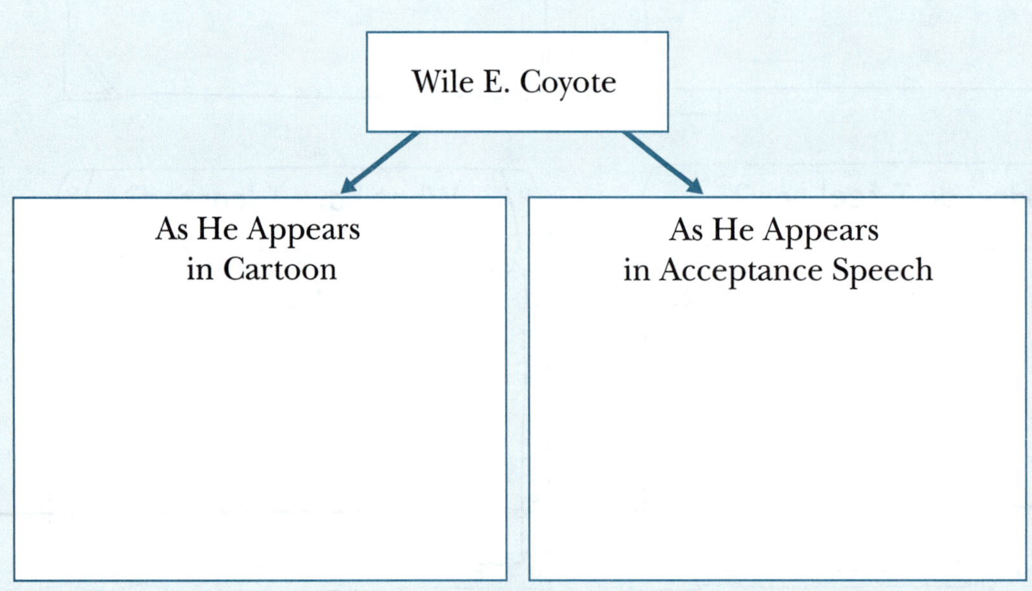

On Behalf of Coyotes Everywhere

Acceptance Speech by Diane Robitaille

I accept this award on behalf of coyotes everywhere! I thank all of you at the ACME Supply Company for this honour. Those of you who know me know that Wile E. Coyote is a humble coyote with a genius for invention. I do not let failure stop me from trying again and again. I learn from my mistakes and always have a plan ready. I am a coyote of few words but deep thoughts.

During the past 50 years, I have tried 1000 times to catch Roadrunner. I have tested 600 ACME products. With each test, I learn more about Roadrunner's weaknesses. With each test, I am one day closer to success.

As many of you know, Roadrunner enjoys annoying and teasing me. Its shrill beep is designed to drive me crazy. It laughs at my failures and sticks its tongue out at my greatest efforts. I will not give up. I will not rest until Roadrunner has been caught.

For 50 years, the ACME Supply Company has provided me with every item a clever coyote needs. I thank you for that support. I know who my friends are, just as I know my enemies.

I have worked hard with little reward. One reward I have taken away is knowledge: of safety procedures, equipment and products, weapons and booby traps. I have learned how to fly and how to fall, how to swim and how to sink, and how to get back up, over and over, and begin again and again.

I am proud of the creativity I've shown, as well as my persistence. That the ACME Supply Company would honour my inventiveness and determination with this award makes me so much prouder. I will remain a loyal customer of the ACME Supply Company as long as Roadrunner runs free!

Thank you.

Critical Thinking   *Making Connections*

1. Take **ten** minutes to think about the following point:

   - The author of "On Behalf of Coyotes Everywhere" tries to make
     Wile E. Coyote look good. She shows his best side and puts a positive
     spin on things that really happened to Wile E.

2. In your notebook, record at least **two** ways the author makes Wile E.
   look good, but still manages to reflect the actual cartoon character.
   You'll need to make connections between the acceptance speech and
   the cartoon show. Below is a sample answer.

> I know from watching the cartoons that Wile E. has had a lot of accidents.
> The author takes that idea and twists it around and has Wile E. claim that he knows
> safety procedures, which makes Wile E. look good. It's probably true that Wile E. does
> have a lot of experience with dangerous situations!

3. With a small group, take **ten** minutes to discuss your ideas.

Oral Communication   *Telling Life Stories*

1. Work with a partner on the following activity. Each of you should
   choose **one** of the following viewpoints:

   - Imagine you're Wile E. Coyote as shown in the cartoon.
     Tell your partner your life story.

   - Imagine you're Wile E. Coyote as shown in the speech.
     Tell your partner your life story.

2. With your partner, discuss how these stories are different.

Extending: With your partner, choose another fictional character from
books, TV shows, movies, or cartoons. Create an acceptance speech that
character might give after getting some award. Remember to show the
character's best side.

     On Behalf of Coyotes Everywhere   **129**

1. Look over the list of words in the chart below.

Word	Have I Heard or Seen the Word Before?	What Do I think the Word Means?
behalf		
humble		
genius		
booby traps		
persistence		

2. Find and <u>underline</u> these words in the selection. Check how the words are used.

3. Complete both columns of the chart.

4. Check a dictionary to see if your definition for each word is correct. Check to see if your definition works in the selection.

Working out Meaning

If you don't know the meaning of a word, you can:

- Think about the words you know that are **around** the new word.
- Think about the **parts** of the new word.
- Think about how the new word connects to the **topic**.

During Reading

Reflect on what this fictional wanted poster tells you about the time and place it is set. Is the person who is "wanted" a villain or a hero? Make notes about your ideas in the margin beside the poster.

Wanted Poster by Vesna Krstanovic

> ### Goals at a Glance
> reading between the lines • writing a story

Reading Between the Lines

When you are **reading between the lines**, you often need to figure out the meaning **behind** what the writer is saying.

- Ask Yourself: Why did the writer tell me that? What does the writer mean here?
- Think about the clues that the writer is giving about events and characters.

Use the image as well as the text on the wanted poster to help you answer these questions. Support your answers.

1. What do you think the **setting** (time and place) is for this wanted poster?

2. What is happening to the people who created this poster?

3. What is happening to the person who is wanted in this poster?

4. Do you think "Granny" Gail is a hero or a villain? Why?

1. Think about **two** questions you would like to ask "Granny" Gail Gallagher.
   Write the questions below.

   Question 1: ____

   ____

   Question 2: ____

   ____

2. Exchange your questions with a partner's questions and answer them in
   role as "Granny" Gail.

   ____

   ____

C **Writing**   *A Story*

- **Perspective** is the point of view from which events are told.

- Each person may have a different perspective about the same events.

---

1. Choose **one** of the following **perspectives**:

   - the person who is trying to capture
     "Granny" Gail Gallagher

   - "Granny" Gail Gallagher

2. Think about the story this person would
   tell. You'll need to expand on the details
   given in the wanted poster. Use the outline
   to help you. Write your ideas in your
   notebook.

3. Use your ideas to write the story of the
   person you chose.

4. Share your story with a partner.

Outline

Characters (Who?)
—
—
—

Setting (Where and when?)
—

Conflict (What's the problem?)
—

Plot (What happens?)
—
—

Ending (How is the problem
        solved?)
—

UNIT 5 WRAP-UP

1. Check off the critical thinking activities you completed during this unit:

   ❑ Making Comparisons (page 117)
   ❑ Forming Opinions (page 123)
   ❑ Making Connections (page 129)
   ❑ Reading Between the Lines (page 132)

2. Describe how **one** of these activities helped you increase your understanding of the selections in this unit.

   ____

   ____

   ____

Project Idea   *Telling Stories*

Step 1. Think about the selections and formats in this unit and how they each tell a story.

Step 2. Look for other myths, articles, diagrams, speeches, and wanted posters, as well as other formats that tell stories (diaries, Web pages, posters, ads, photos, and so on).

Step 3. Choose **one** of these selections and think about the story it tells. Use your imagination to expand on the details and develop the story.

Step 4. Retell the story of that selection to a small group. Remember to think about the perspective or point of view of the original selection. Do you want to keep the same perspective when you retell the story?

Step 5. Share the original selection with your group. Tell them how it inspired the story you told.

What do you do to help you work out the meaning of a word you don't know? For example, the word <u>whereabouts</u> is used in the selection "Wanted!" Here's one way you could work out the meaning of the word <u>whereabouts</u>.

Step 1. Think about the words that are around the word **whereabouts**.

Step 2. Think about the parts of the word **whereabouts**: **Where** and **abouts.**

Step 3. Finally, put together your thoughts about the word **whereabouts**. You'll probably be able to work out that **whereabouts** is "the place where someone or something is." In this case, that someone is "Granny" Gail.

Step 4. After reading, look up the word in the dictionary to check your understanding.

Note: You may not need to follow all of these steps every time you read a new word. Sometimes, just by completing one of these steps, you'll be able to work out the meaning. Give these steps a try the next time you come across a word you don't know.

WANTED
FOR SELLING SECRETS TO THE ENEMY, SPYING, AND HUNTING FISH AND DEER OUT OF SEASON.

Also wanted for supplying captured enemy soldiers with food, maps, and clothing and aiding their escape. Often seen with a white horse, near battlefields, caring for the wounded. Sometimes hides out in local orphanages or poorhouses, acting like the cook.

Contact Governor Gruesome with news of Gail's <u>whereabouts</u>.

abbreviation: the shortened form of a word (for example, **Sat.** is the abbreviation for **Saturday**)

adjective: a word that describes a noun or pronoun (for example, great, red, smooth)

adverb: a word that modifies a verb, an adjective, or another adverb. It tells the reader more about the action (for example, the boat moved slowly, the brightly shining star)

apostrophe: the punctuation mark (') used to indicate a missing or dropped letter, or to indicate ownership of something, as in can't or Cindy's cat

audience: anyone who will be reading or viewing a text

brainstorm: to contribute ideas on one topic in a group

by-line: the information after the title

capital letters: the uppercase letters of the alphabet

caption: the writing beside or below an image that tells you what the image is about

comma: the punctuation mark (,) used to show a slight pause in a sentence

compound word: a word made up of two or more words (for example, sweatshirt, goldfish, doghouse)

conclusion: the concluding sentence or a paragraph that sums up earlier information

context: the words or sentences around a word that help show its meaning

contraction: a word formed by joining two other words (for example, I'll, he's)

diagram: a picture with labels used to show or explain something

dialogue: the lines a character speaks

draw conclusions: to use information in the text to make decisions about the characters or events

elaborate descriptions: detailed descriptions used to create interest

exclamation mark: an exclamation mark (**!**) ends a sentence that has strong feeling in it

fact: information that can be proven true

future tense: the tense of a verb that tells about something that will happen

idiom: an expression that has a different meaning than the dictionary definitions of the individual words

index: a detailed list of topics located in the back of a book

infer (make inferences): to use clues in the text or "read between the lines" to make an educated guess about what is happening in the text

KWL chart: a chart recording what you **K**now, **W**ant to Know, and have **L**earned

message: the information, idea, or lesson a writer is trying to give the reader

noun: a word that names a person, place, thing, or idea

opinion: a judgment or view of something

paragraph: a group of sentences about one topic or idea

past tense: the verb tense that tells about something that happened in the past

period: the punctuation mark (.) used at the end of a statement

predict: to make an educated guess about what will happen in a text

prefix: the part of a word added to the beginning of a root word to change its meaning (for example, unhappy, reread)

present tense: the verb tense that tells you what is happening now

previewing: looking over a text before reading it

pronoun: a word used in place of a noun (for example, me, you, I)

proper noun: a word that names a particular person, place, or thing, (for example, Nancy, Vancouver, Stanley Cup)

purpose: the reason a text was created (for example, to persuade someone to do or buy something)

question mark: the punctuation mark (?) used at the end of a question

quotation marks: the marks (" ") used to indicate that someone is speaking

sentence: a group of words that expresses a complete thought

skim: to quickly read parts of a text to get a sense of what it is about

suffix: the part of a word added to the end of the base word to change the meaning (for example, joyful, teacher)

summary: to make a brief statement giving the main points of a text

synonym: a word that has the same or almost the same meaning as another word

topic sentence: a statement that tells what a paragraph is about

verb: a word that expresses an action, feeling, or state of being

vivid verbs: strong, descriptive verbs

INDEX

Bold numbers indicate Strategy boxes and Close-Up pages.

ACKNOWLEDGMENTS

Text Credits

2-3 *The Best of the World's Stupidest Signs*, collected by Michael O'Mara, Michael O'Mara Books Limited. **6-11** Reprinted by permission of Robert Piotrowski. **17-18** "Step on No Pets," "Stack Cats," and "The Artist" from PALINDROMANIA! by Jon Agee. Copyright © 2002 by Jon Agee. Reprinted by permission of Farrar, Straus and Giroux, LLC. **23** "The Hardest Thing" by Judith Viorst. From SAD UNDERWEAR AND OTHER COMPLICATIONS. Published by Atheneum Books for Young Readers (USA). An imprint of Simon & Schuster Children's Publishing Division. Text Copyright © 1995 by Judith Viorst. Reprinted by permission of Lescher & Lescher, Ltd. All rights reserved. **24** Text copyright © 2003 by James Stevenson. Used by permission of HarperCollins Publishers. **25** Copyright © 1996 by Shel Silverstein and Evil Eye Music, Inc. Reprinted by permission of HarperCollins Publishers and Edite Kroll Literary Agency Inc. **32-33** Nelson Text Copyright © 2005 Nelson, a division of Thomson Canada Ltd. **39-41** Vision Quest by Ron Geyshick. Reprinted by permission of Judith Doyle. **45-46, 61** From *Pluralist: An Anthology of Creative Writing*, Greater Essex County Public Secondary Schools. Reprinted by permission. **50-53** From *Super Sleuth: Twelve Solve-It-Yourself Mysteries* by Jackie Vivelo, Penguin Group (USA) Inc. **56** Reprinted with permission of Pleasant Company Publications from *The Quiz Book* © 1999 by American Girl, LLC. **63 bottom** Courtesy of CBC and Alliance Atlantis. **64 top** Courtesy of APTN and Summerhill Entertainment. **64 bottom** Courtesy of APTN and Catalyst Entertainment (Productions) Inc. **65** Courtesy of Apartment 11 Productions and YTV Canada, Inc. **71-73** From: *Made in Canada: 101 Amazing Achievements.* Copyright © 2003 by Beverly Spencer. All rights reserved. Reprinted by permission of Scholastic Canada Ltd. **77-81** Copyright © 2005 Nancy Christoffer. **85** Courtesy of YTV and Apartment 11. **87-88** Adapted with permission of Sterling Publishing Co., NY, NY from GROSS ME OUT! 50 NASTY PROJECTS TO DISGUST YOUR FRIENDS & REPULSE YOUR FAMILY by Sloppy Joe Rhatigan and Revoltin' Rain Newcomb. Illustrated by Clay Meyer, © 2004 by Lark Books, a Division of Sterling Publishing Co., Inc. Illustrations © 2004 by Clay Meyer. **92-93** Reprinted by permission of Pippa Wysong. **98-100** Adapted from "All About Bats" from *Creature Features* by Anita Ganeri, illustrated by Steve Fricker, 1997. Reprinted by permission of Marshall Editions. **104-106** Nelson Text Copyright © 2005 Nelson, a division of Thomson Canada Ltd. **111-115** Text copyright © Kiri Te Kanawa 1989, illustrations copyright © Michael Foreman 1989. Reproduced by permission of Chrysalis Children's Books, an imprint of Chrysalis Books Group Plc. **120-122** "Oak Island Money Pit" from *Hidden Treasure: Amazing Stories of Discovery* by Tina Holdcroft. Published by Annick Press 2003. Reprinted with permission. **127-128** Copyright © 2005 Diane Robitaille. For information contact D. Robitaille at 39 Sealcove Drive, Toronto, Ontario, M9C 2C7, 416 695 1738. **131** Copyright © 2005 Diane Robitaille. For information contact D. Robitaille at 39 Sealcove Drive, Toronto, Ontario, M9C 2C7, 416 695 1738.

Visual Credits

63 top Courtesy of CBC, **63 bottom** Courtesy of CBC and Alliance Atlantis. **64 top** Courtesy of APTN and Summerhill Entertainment, **64 bottom** Courtesy of APTN and Catalyst Entertainment (Productions) Inc. **65** Courtesy of Apartment 11 Productions and YTV Canada, Inc. **71-72** © IMAX Corporation. **77** First National/The Kobal Collection. **78** © Sunset Boulevard/CORBIS/MAGMA. **79** Castle Rock/Shangri-La Entertainment/The Kobal Collection. **80 left** The Ronald Grant Archive. **80 right** Touchstone/Jerry Bruckheimer Inc./The Kobal Collection. **88 top** Bob Elsdale/The Image Bank/Getty Images. **88 bottom** Joe McDonald/OSF/firstlight.ca. **92** photoresearchers/firstlight.ca.

Illustrations

6 Vesna Krstanovic. **29, 43, 52, 53, 94, 102, 105, 116, 117, 124, 125, 126, 133 top** Crowle Art Group. **32, 33** Ken Dewar. **41** Heather Collins. **46** Tina Holdcroft. **50** Sharon Matthews. **127,** Andrew Breithaupt.